6.50

D1740420

Civilized Oppression and Moral Relations

Civilized Oppression and Moral Relations

Victims, Fallibility, and the Moral Community

By
Jean Harvey

Edited by
Antonio Calcagno

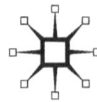

CIVILIZED OPPRESSION AND MORAL RELATIONS

Copyright © Jean Harvey, 2015.

All rights reserved.

First published in 2015 by
PALGRAVE MACMILLAN®
in the United States—a division of St. Martin's Press LLC,
175 Fifth Avenue, New York, NY 10010.

Where this book is distributed in the UK, Europe and the rest of the world,
this is by Palgrave Macmillan, a division of Macmillan Publishers Limited,
registered in England, company number 785998, of Houndmills,
Basingstoke, Hampshire RG21 6XS.

Palgrave Macmillan is the global academic imprint of the above companies
and has companies and representatives throughout the world.

Palgrave® and Macmillan® are registered trademarks in the United States,
the United Kingdom, Europe and other countries.

ISBN: 978–1–137–50699–3

Library of Congress Cataloging-in-Publication Data

Harvey, Jean, 1955–
    Civilized oppression and moral relations : victims, fallibility and the
    moral community / by Jean Harvey; edited by Antonio Calcagno.
        pages cm
    Includes bibliographical references and index.
    ISBN 978–1–137–50699–3—ISBN 1–137–50699–7
        1. Oppression (Psychology)—Moral and ethical aspects. 2. Liberty—
    Philosophy. 3. Equality—Philosophy. 4. Social justice—Philosophy.
    I. Calcagno, Antonio, 1969– II. Title.

HM1266.H373 2015
303.3'72—dc23   2014040015

A catalogue record of the book is available from the British Library.

Design by Newgen Knowledge Works (P) Ltd., Chennai, India.

First edition: April 2015

10 9 8 7 6 5 4 3 2 1

Contents

Acknowledgments

I am grateful for the assistance of Antonio Calcagno in preparing this book for final publication.

Reworked material drawn from earlier studies has been incorporated into this monograph. I thank the publishers for their permission to reproduce some of that material here in this new book:

1. "Victims, Resistance, and Civilized Oppression," in *Symposium: Responsibility for Resisting Oppression*: cocontributors, Bernard Boxill and Thomas E. Hill; commentator, Sarah Buss; *Journal of Social Philosophy* 41, no. 1 (Spring 2010), 13–27.
2. "Authentic Social Justice and the Far Reaches of 'The Private Sphere,'" *Social Philosophy Today* 26 (2011), 9–22.
3. "Moral Solidarity and Empathetic Understanding: The Moral Value and Scope of the Relationship," in *Special Issue on Solidarity*, *Journal of Social Philosophy*, ed. Carol Gould and Sally Scholz, 38, no. 1 (2007), 22–37.
4. "The Burden of Securing Social Justice: Institutions, Individuals, and Moral Action," *Social Philosophy Today* 22 (2007), 137–152.

CHAPTER 1

Introduction: Further Discussions of Civilized Oppression

In *The Atrocity Paradigm*[1] Claudia Card discusses genocide, war rape, torture, and spousal and child abuse as cases of "atrocities." They are "uncontroversially evil," they deserve "priority of attention," and the "core features of evils tend to be writ large in the case of atrocities, making them easier to identify and appreciate."[2] (The ease of identification is a major difference between these cases and the phenomena of civilized oppression. It is much harder to recognize the latter.) When directed to members of some group because of their membership in the group, it becomes systematic and an instance of violent oppression, and the examples Card cites have been (and still are) used to terrorize and oppress certain groups. The moral urgency of tackling such oppression is obvious. Nonetheless, I think it would be a major error to collectively tackle only such shockingly violent forms of oppression.

"Civilized oppression" is a phrase I coined some years ago[3] to refer to oppression that involves neither violence, nor the use of law. It is systematic and disadvantages and demeans members of certain groups and in Western societies it is pervasive. The phenomena involved are routinely trivialized, given their subtle nature, yet both their effects and their nonconsequentialist implications are highly significant. My first book, *Civilized Oppression*, focuses on the most central goals: analyzing what is involved in such oppression, making such oppression more recognizable, explaining why it is far more important morally than first appears, and uncovering the underlying principles that account for its immorality.

The key focus in this second book is on the moral relations between the key players: victims, agents of civilized oppression, and bystanders. (By "victim" I refer simply to someone at the receiving end of such oppression and someone, therefore, morally wronged. No image or stereotype is implied.) To keep the work here as self-contained as possible, this first chapter contains some key points about civilized oppression worked on in my first book.

There are important differences between civilized oppression (at least, toward one end of the spectrum of civilized oppression) and more dramatic forms that involve violence. I say "at one end of the spectrum" because civilized oppression itself covers a range of phenomena containing some interesting moral distinctions, some of which carry implications for the moral status of the contributing agents.

I am particularly interested in the most subtle cases, since they are the most underexamined, although they reflect powerful forces that routinely derail lives. Here, more than with any other form of oppression, thinking about the moral role of the contributing agents involves thinking about their ability to make fine-grained perceptions, particularly about their own long-standing habits of action. Some socialized habits contribute greatly to subtle but powerfully effective civilized oppression, but the relevant self-awareness requires a level of perceptual skill that involves commitment over time, not simply goodwill, good intentions, and sincere beliefs about the wrongness of discrimination, exploitation, and marginalization.

Here too the stereotype of the agent as "the enemy" (readily justified in cases of violent oppression and some of the more transparent cases of civilized oppression) can be misleading for more than one reason. Sometimes, in fact, contributions to civilized oppression are actually motivated by basically good intentions (e.g., when someone routinely "blames the victim" of some wrongful harm by pointing to something the victim did—and so could avoid doing—with the hope of protecting the victim from similar harms in the future).

A number of these differences are relevant to our conceptions of the key players and so too to what the relationships should be. This matters, since distorted relationships, I argue, lie at the heart of civilized oppression. It is in the very nature of this type of oppression that much of what is morally wrong is not accounted for in terms of material harm (although such harm predictably follows from what is wrong). Thinking about civilized oppression leads us to questions about the relationships that typically hold between those involved and the relationships that should hold, and although the consequences of actions clearly matter a great deal, analyzing the immorality of this kind of oppression solely in terms of the "consequences" of this or that action does not get to the heart of the matter. We need to explore the moral relations involved.

How can actions that seem completely trivial constitute oppression? Consider an example readily found in daily life. Suppose that those in the more powerful position are comfortable chatting with members of one group but not with those of another. Suppose that the powerful men are comfortable talking informally with other men, but far less so with women. It seems at first a purely personal matter, but it can in fact disadvantage members of the excluded group, both practically and motivationally. They do not receive the timely bits of information and quick tips members of the other group receive; they miss the short anecdote about the new manager that makes the person seem more approachable; and they don't hear the occasional, spontaneous word of praise of encouragement. They miss out on all the richness of the well-disposed, casual encounter. It also means that the socially better positioned are unlikely to know those individuals as well as they do the people they chat with, and in a society where connections can affect success, this can make a difference. What seem like acts of commission or omission of no significance can function in powerful ways.

With all types of oppression the victims have a moral primacy for more than one reason. In cases of violent oppression their suffering demands moral attention and strong action. It is physical suffering that, in principle at least, is highly visible even if committed behind closed doors. It is so blatant and so evil that others cannot turn away from it in good faith. Another reason for the moral primacy of victims is that there are less visible aspects even to this type of oppression. The psychological evil that accompanies such physical suffering has been well documented by prisoners in Nazi concentration camps, by battered wives, by physically abused children (often recounted when adults). Children sexually assaulted by priests suffered terribly in physical ways, but they also suffered psychologically when their priest turned into a monster in front of them, when their own parents refused to believe them when they tried to convey their terror and pain, when they were shunned as liars, or at best obsessed with distasteful fantasies or calumnies. They found themselves trapped in social structures that simply dismissed their reports and refused to see their nightmare. Victims of civilized oppression have an even more crucial role to play in getting the phenomena known. There are, by definition, no blatantly violent actions to see, nothing to arouse any deep moral concern in "observers." Even the agents of the oppression typically do not strike us as immoral, let alone evil. In some cases they are even transparently well intentioned toward the victims they oppress.[4] We can learn about this form of oppression only from the victims themselves (as Laurence Thomas and Elizabeth Spelman urge us to do).

So what is the nature of the relationship, or rather, what relationship should hold, between these victims and the agents of this kind of oppression? Some of the basic points center around fallibility as a shared feature of agents; it is obviously unreasonable to expect moral perfection, either in others or ourselves. Given that civilized oppression involves phenomena that are far less visible than those found in violent oppression, it is understandable (as has been noted earlier) that many contributing agents are unaware of their role, notably so at the far end of the civilized oppression spectrum where the agents are literally unaware of the habitual and fine-grained actions they engage in. Their oversights call for some empathy, given that they are ones we all share even if in nonoppressive contexts.

Also those agents who are committed to learning about the oppression, primarily by listening to its victims, are engaged in a process of increasing awareness, both of the nature of what is wrong and of their role in it. Acquiring empathetic understanding of the oppression and acquiring an increasing awareness of one's habitual actions both involve gradual processes. Errors of judgment and oversights are to be expected on occasion. Although the demand for perfection is not one we hear in these situations, it is nonetheless hovering in the practice of condemning someone outright as soon as they make one error of judgment. Victims who are long-term oppressed may understandably have a fairly short fuse when it comes to some kinds of mistakes made by the non-oppressed who would support them, but condemning them in ways that dismiss them permanently as potential fellow fighters in the cause is not only unwise, it is, more to the point, unfair.

When the privileged non-oppressed do try to learn about civilized oppression and what they themselves are doing to support it, when they begin to make changes in their actions, it was pointed out that they usually pay a price for this disloyalty to their socially advantaged group. The costs they pay are as often overlooked as the harms inflicted on the victims of civilized oppression, especially early on in any social change of common and oppressive practices when few of the privileged step out of line. It can be morally appropriate for the victims to be grateful for those who begin to make changes and begin to voice the concerns.

So, unlike situations of violent oppression, I am claiming that victims of civilized oppression have good reasons for being sympathetic to the type and degree of fallibility found in many agents of civilized oppression. These agents are typically not the enemy in any classic sense and the failings of many of them are shared by the victims.

In chapter 2, I examine the traditional claim that gratitude is an appropriate response only to acts of benevolence that are not morally owed and only where the motive is that of trying to help. Otherwise gratitude is uncalled for.

I challenge this tradition in two ways, situating my discussion in relation to civilized oppression. First, I critique what I call the "moral atomism" typically involved, that is, thinking that we can assess a moral situation by looking just at the key players (in this case, the benevolent person and the one helped). Life is lived in relationships: some personal, some at the societal level where power structures can affect both the moral description and the assessment of some situation or incident. (Feminist philosophy fully supports this insight.) Second, I challenge the core of the traditional position and argue that sometimes there may be good reasons for being grateful to someone who fulfills a moral obligation.

Although feminist philosophy rejects the moral atomism of the standard position on gratitude, the actual core of the position (that gratitude is never called for in response to a morally obligatory action) seems to be generally accepted, and in addition, the role of the relationships involved is sometimes oversimplified. As a point of departure from this trend, I argue that it can sometimes be appropriate for the oppressed to be grateful to the thoughtful members of privileged groups—the breakaway "heroes"—who contribute to ending oppression, even though such contributions are morally owed.

The chapter also concludes that appropriate relationships of gratitude are part of what can bring to life a notion of a moral community, and if gratitude is seen as inherently demeaning, then something is very wrong with the underlying conception of a moral community and the relationships within it. (This is one of the pointers along the way in considering just a few implications of the book's findings for a reconception of moral community.)

In chapter 3, I explore a morally rich notion of solidarity and the relationships it promotes. In doing so, I argue for the role of empathetic understanding in the moral response to civilized oppression (a position generally accepted in feminist philosophy), but introduce two caveats that extend the role of moral solidarity in controversial ways.

There is currently no agreed-upon meaning given to "moral solidarity," so I explore the question, how should we conceive of moral solidarity if we are to reach a morally rich conception of that bond, something morally worth striving for? After rejecting two apparently plausible candidates, I examine the relationship between members of an oppressed group and relatively powerful, non-oppressed others to see what can this suggests about a desirable form of moral solidarity.

That relationship is much discussed in feminist literature and the call for empathetic understanding of the oppressed by the privileged is often central (e.g., Elizabeth Spelman urges the privileged to become "apprentices" to the oppressed in order to understand their situation and experience,[5] and Laurence Thomas calls for the privileged to show "moral deference" to the oppressed in understanding their experiences and pain).[6]

Building the relationship of moral solidarity around empathetic understanding is a move I fully endorse. That said, I argue for two caveats. The first is that we should beware of allowing paradigm cases to set false boundaries on the role of empathetic understanding. Usually we learn about the situations of the oppressed by listening empathetically to their stories and protests and entering into a relationship of moral solidarity with them. I make the case that we can be in moral solidarity with victims of oppression who are not able to articulate their stories in the standard sense (including systematically oppressed animals).

The second caveat is even more controversial, since it relies on the claim that at one end of the civilized oppression spectrum (involving the most subtle cases), agents contributing to the oppression have an understandable lack of awareness of their role. Is it, then, ever appropriate for victims of civilized oppression to be in a relationship of empathetic understanding, and even, correlatively, moral solidarity, with agents who contribute to their oppression (a complete reversal of the direction of moral solidarity in the paradigm cases)? I explore whether we can make moral sense of being firmly against the oppression, but not against the oppressors.

Akin to the previous chapter, this chapter concludes that appropriate relationships of moral solidarity can morally enrich the notion of a moral community. It is one more piece collected along the way that will be drawn into the final chapter.

In chapter 4, I look at the relationship between civilized oppression, moral community, and resistance. Feminist philosophy has much to say about resisting oppression, but as with a number of other issues, overgeneralizing about oppression leads to misleading conclusions about resistance.

For example, many agents of civilized oppression, unlike those employing terror and violence, are not easily identifiable as the enemy. Also, Ann Cudd speaks of oppressors as people who "intend to act in order to continue or intensify the oppression of a social group,"[7] but this too is overgeneralized: agents of civilized oppression often have no such intention, and at one end of the civilized oppression spectrum at least, understandably no awareness of their role or their contributing actions. Again, in paradigm cases we think of resistance as fighting against the oppressor, the enemy, with whatever resources can be marshalled, but our attitude toward those contributing to civilized oppression may be justifiably rather different, even while realizing that the oppression itself has to end.

In the rest of the chapter I look at two nonstandard forms of resistance that are especially relevant to civilized oppression.

The first involves educational initiatives. Thinking of education, both formal and informal, as a form of resistance is unusual, but apt in the case of civilized oppression.

I examine the grounds for claiming that victims may even have a prima facie obligation to "educate"—to speak up, protest, explain, and inform the non-oppressed, a claim clearly implied, for example, in Laurence Thomas's work.[8] While supporting that prima facie obligation as an imperfect duty, I also argue for a central, but nonobvious, limitation on it.

The more obvious moral limitations are, first, a plausible looking right to protect oneself from serious risks, and second, an equally plausible-looking right to guard one's personal resources, especially time and energy. The less obvious constraint argued for here is the right to protect one's self-identity from wholesale manipulation, strangely from the non-oppressed most concerned to diminish the oppression. Their continual "moral deference" (Thomas's phrase) to the victims of oppression involves stepping back and letting the victims, as the experts, speak about the oppressive situation, asking the victims to explain the impact and effects, avoiding the risk of paternalism by expecting the victims to protest their own harms, and so on. This not only affects the personal time and energies of the victims, it can coercively define their whole self-identity as "a victim of oppression." What begins as deference can transform itself into a kind of second order oppression, however unintended.

This is a different type of psychological damage from that typically cited in connection with victims of oppression,[9] and furthermore, the unwitting agents of this harm are not the oppressors (those typically cited as the ones contributing to the psychological damage), but those privileged non-oppressed most respectful of the victims and most concerned to diminish civilized oppression.

The second nonstandard mode of resistance discussed is that of building certain kinds of relationships with the oppressors at one end of the civilized oppression spectrum: those in positions of privilege who are goodwilled and generally benevolent, but unaware of their long-standing, socialized habits that systematically contribute to the oppression. These initiatives on the part of the victims are not undertaken in the spirit of appeasement, but as acts of moral agency and membership in the moral community.

A society where we find pervasive forms of oppression has not achieved social justice. In Western societies, civilized oppression is still pervasive, but it is inherently difficult to perceive.

Another feature of civilized oppression is that its very nature leads us to think about individuals in specific situations and interactions (although the relevance of concrete specifics does not mean that moral principles have no bearing). There are irreducibly "individual" contributions to the situations and patterns of civilized oppression. Correlatively there are irreducibly individual contributions involved in a society free of civilized oppression, contributions that are not arrived at by any trickle-down effects of major social institutions. They are some of the constitutive elements of a socially just society (or one where social justice is an ongoing goal) and no perfection of major social institutions can substitute for them.

The notion of such irreducibly individual contributions is a very different matter from a misguided "moral atomism" and the distinction between these two concepts will be explained in this chapter.

In mainstream philosophy it is a strong methodological tradition to try to reach insights about social justice by arguing for what social justice would involve if we were starting with a blank slate and organizing a fresh and new society. It is also still a dominant tradition to conceive of social justice on the distributive model and, further, to construe justice as all about the major social institutions. Each of these three aspects of this traditional approach make it yet more difficult to take civilized oppression seriously. In the first place, thinking solely about what a just society should be like will not yield the insights about civilized oppression that we need if we are to tackle it. The approach is too coarse grained to come to grips with subtle forms of injustice. Second, while the distributive model of social justice lends itself to talking about inequalities and unfairness in regard to material assets like money, matters to do with relationships are poorly handled on this model. We can, in principle at least, look at how much wealth each has, but looking at each individual—as an individual—cannot, even in principle, tell us what relationships they are embedded in, nor can it tell us what their life-situation is with respect to what I call "relationship power" (the power they have in their various relationships). Relationships are not things that are accumulated as holdings by an individual, yet abuse of relationship power is a major source of civilized oppression. Third, construing social justice solely in terms of major social institutions is a "top-down" conception of social justice: if we get the basic social institutions right, then justice will trickle down to individual lives.[10] As important as the basic social institutions are, it remains the case that if we understand the phenomena involved in civilized oppression, we can see that some components of social justice necessarily arise "from the ground up," from individuals and their situations, actions, relationships, and interactions, and from moral considerations that apply directly to them.

So, in chapter 5, I highlight one way in which civilized oppression—a form of social injustice—involves such irreducibly individual components. Interactions between individuals—not involving violence—make up one of the primary sites for civilized oppression when the individuals involved differ in status and social power. When such differences are socially supported, there exists an often unquestioned difference in what I call relationship power and this can be readily misused. I will make a case for what I call "interactional justice" and for some of the moral principles involved. This type of justice cannot be safely arrived at by some top-down effect from major social institutions, something that becomes clear once we understand what goes wrong in interactions constituting interactional *in*justice.

In a whole range of cases that fall within civilized oppression, what is amiss in the interactions passes under the radar screen. At one end of the spectrum of situations involved in civilized oppression, what is involved is too fine grained to be blocked via explicit regulations, whether state laws or the policies of specific institutions (even though what is going wrong has striking effects on those on the receiving end). By the very nature of the case, initiatives have to be taken by the individuals themselves in these situations. Interactional justice is a component of social justice that is grounded far more in the moral relations that should hold between individuals than it is in the idea of distributing assets.

Chapter 6 examines a second way in which irreducibly individual contributions play a key role in civilized oppression and, correlatively, in a socially just society, or one where we aim to radically reduce civilized oppression. Here it is not interactions between individuals that are involved, but the mental lives of individuals.

It is commonly held that only a tyrannical government would try to form, monitor, and control not only actions, but the mental lives of its citizens. Actions are "public," but the mind is utterly "private" and therefore no one's concern but the individual's and something that falls outside of the sphere of social justice.

Joseph Tussman critiques this standard position, arguing that government should be concerned about the minds of citizens and involved in the education of the youth of the nation for consequentialist reasons: thoughts and attitudes spill out into actions and these consequences are not private.[11]

However, I argue for the moral significance of thoughts and attitudes, separate from any consequences (especially actions) that may result from them. Distorted relationships between individuals lie at the heart of civilized oppression and the authenticity of these relationships depends not only on "visible actions," but on the attitudes and thoughts of the individuals. Actions can often be described at different levels, from a primitively behavioral (describing what I call the visible actions) to the more usual, richer description that often does imply certain attitudes on the part of the agent. For example, to say that someone "extends her sympathy to him in his time of grief and loss," it's not enough that "she goes to him and says that she has heard of his loss and is sorry to hear of it" if, in fact, she is so malicious that inside she is savoring his misery. It may be an accurate description of the visible actions, but it is not enough to count as "extending her sympathy to him," since in this unusual case she has no sympathy to extend.

I make the case that authentic moral relations holding between individuals are essential if social justice is to be more than an illusion, and that certain attitudes are constitutive of what I call "authentic social justice" even though a government cannot—and should not—try to somehow "force" individuals to hold such attitudes and beliefs. (Other forms of influence, such as educational initiatives, as Tussman notes, may be morally acceptable or even called for.) I argue, then, that authentic social justice involves elements of the mental life that can only be contributed by individuals as individuals. They are, in that sense, "irreducibly individual." This conception of authentic social justice and the arguments in support of it highlight the role of moral relations in thinking about social justice.

The final chapter in the book examines the relationship between the victims of civilized oppression and those who contribute to this kind of oppression. In particular, from the victims' perspective, how should the relationship be viewed and what should it be? Given the moral primacy of the plight of the victims of oppression, this relationship is perhaps the most critical to examine more closely. The second part of the chapter will then consider in what sense that moral relationship can form part of a morally sound conception of a moral community.

With respect to the first part of the chapter, what makes the issue of the moral relationship between victims and contributing agents challenging is precisely the special nature of this type of oppression and the correlated facts about those who contribute to it. Genuine goodwill and general benevolence can exist side by side with no awareness of one's own socialized habits, or indeed those of others, at least the more subtle of them. Also, the tendency to think only of one's own actions obscures how they contribute to cumulative patterns formed by multiple agents, patters that are devastating to the victims. Again, a well-disposed attitude toward those we interact with seems to be simply a matter of well-intentioned sociability and perhaps basic kindness; few think of their role in social structures that consolidate power and status in ways that

marginalize nonmembers of "the group." There are many such phenomena that have special significance in the workings of civilized oppression
and which are therefore relevant to this central relationship.

Quite a range of the oppressors' actions, habits, and oversights may
reasonably be viewed sympathetically by the victims, in that they themselves may often have the same experiences, perform analogous actions,
or fail to notice the same types of things. Only their social context
blocks the potentially oppressive effects (and sometimes it does not; for
example, they can be oppressive to members of other groups). In the
case of violent oppression committed by competent adults, it is far more
straightforward to see the oppressor as the enemy, the one we need to
fight against with all we have. With civilized oppression, many agents
lack the usual, striking features of character that mark them as villains.
In fact, some contributing agents would enter into physically dangerous
situations to rescue another, and some contributing agents are actively
striving to diminish the oppression or trying to protect the victims from
further harm (as in certain types of "blaming the victim" patterns).

A consequentialist approach to asking what moral relations should
hold between the victims of civilized oppression and the contributing
agents, one that focuses on straightforward effects, will point to rather
different conclusions from that of asking what the moral relations should
be in their own right. I look at some work that does rest primarily or
ultimately on considering consequences, but will argue that consequen-
tialism here does not come to grips with the special features of civilized
oppression, nor does it do justice to the nature of the moral life lived in
community and to the prima facie obligations involved.

With respect to the second part of the chapter, a number of implications for the nature of a moral community are examined. (This part
of the final chapter is more exploratory than the rest of the work.) It
highlights especially the shared moral fallibility of people with basically
goodwill, including many agents and victims of civilized oppression. The
central question then is, how do we respect and support each other in our
shared fallibility while still striving to lessen civilized oppression? After
all, if we are willing to respect and support only others who are morally
perfect, then there is no possibility of a moral community.

CHAPTER 2

Civilized Oppression and Gratitude

I n this chapter I look at a few central issues that are especially relevant to questions about civilized oppression and gratitude, as a way to begin thinking about the moral relations involved in everyday situations vulnerable to such oppression. I begin by asking what the most commonly held position seems to be with respect to when gratitude is appropriate and when not, and I will also look at the central claim of this fairly standard position and see how it is supposed to be applied to actual situations.

I will also consider the tradition of seeing gratitude as such (not only falsely induced gratitude) as demeaning. Why is it that in this tradition even situations that are seen as justifiably calling for gratitude are thought of as situations to avoid, if at all possible? I will argue that such a blanket condemnation of gratitude is unsound and rests on morally confused notions of what certain moral relations should be.

The Most Standard Position on When Gratitude Is Appropriate

Since the mid-1970s there has been a flurry of philosophical literature on gratitude covering quite a range of issues: whether feelings are an essential part of gratitude, whether there are necessary conditions that must hold before gratitude is appropriate, whether gratitude is really a moral obligation in some circumstances, whether it involves some kind of debt, and whether it is intrinsically demeaning. I begin with the most central question about this literature: what does it have to say about when gratitude is morally appropriate?

Probably the first notable article in recent series on gratitude is Daniel Lyons' "The Odd Debt of Gratitude" (1969).[1] He draws a distinction between what he calls "perfunctory thanks" and "real thanks," claiming that although the former may be due even when the service rendered is the beneficiary's right, real thanks are due only when the service is "really praiseworthy," when in fact no blame would be incurred if the benefactor refrained from helping.[2] His example of a situation where only perfunctory thanks are due is that of someone returning a lost wallet to me.

> I would be expected to say thank you, and even perhaps to offer a nominal reward: yet it would be admirable for the returner to dismiss my thanks, noting accurately that he just did his basic duty. Here is a case where the benefit is clearly my right (having the wallet returned), where failure to return it would be blameworthy.[3]

For some years after Lyons' article, it was typically claimed that gratitude is the proper response not to just *any* benefit received, but only to an act of un-owed benevolence.[4] The very fact that someone is doing what she ought to disqualifies her from being a suitable recipient of gratitude. The assistance given must fall outside of any moral obligation.

Another specified necessary condition widely shared in the same literature has to do with the benefactor's motives. In particular, there is no reason to be grateful if the action is self-interested, if, for example, aid is given in order to look good or with a view to pressuring the beneficiary for help at some later date.[5] Most specify that the benefit must be given precisely in order to help the recipient.[6]

I think there are some problems embedded in these conditions, but let's start by looking at a classic situation where help is given to someone in need. Imagine a homeless person living in destitution and facing hunger nearly every day. Someone walks up to her and gives her food or a little money, with the intention of helping her. It is help given with the right motive (according to the standard position above), so we should expect the recipient to be grateful, shouldn't we? Or should we? Suppose the benefactor is someone who is himself very poor, who has found part-time work as a laborer just a few days before and who therefore has just a tiny bit of money not urgently needed for food and shelter. Contrast this with a benefactor who is clearly a member of the socially elite, someone who has an abundance of wealth not needed for the basics of living. Does it matter who the helper is? In both cases, it is an act of help with the motive of trying to help, so both cases meet the two standard conditions for gratitude being a fitting response.

As mentioned earlier, the answer most often given in the literature as to whether gratitude is appropriate is that, given that the two conditions above hold, the remaining issue is whether the benefactor is morally obligated to help. If so, then gratitude should not be forthcoming, but if the help is not morally owed (and the motive is to help), then other things being equal, a grateful attitude is appropriate. That is to say, there is an assumed connection between gratitude and moral obligation: gratitude can be fitting only if the help is not morally obligatory. This gratitude/non-obligation connection, G/NO for simplicity, is a major target in this chapter.

Returning to our example, is a response of gratitude appropriate in the case of either or both of the helpers? The G/NO principle directs us first to ask if either benefactor has a moral obligation to help the woman. For some ethical theorists, neither of the two has a strict moral duty to help. On a Kantian position, as traditionally interpreted, benevolence is "an imperfect duty," and on conventional interpretations of that notion, this leaves considerable leeway as to when and where to help, while still being morally up to the mark, so to speak. It matters that enough help is given over time, but the actual occasions are not dictated by moral duty. Again, for libertarians, giving help to those in great need is not a moral duty of any kind, not even an "imperfect" duty (at least, not unless their great need is a direct result of someone violating one of their three basic, negative rights, e.g., by stealing their possessions).[7] One may choose to help, but such charity is supererogatory, something over and above any moral duty. There is no moral obligation to give help directly as an individual, nor to cooperate with government schemes to redistribute money from the rich to the poor. Insofar as tax schemes are designed to do this, they are typically characterized by libertarians as forms of theft. Income tax is a form of forced labor where the gains of that labor are snatched from you. Since the key issue here is of there being a moral duty or not, theories such as these would indicate that the recipient would be displaying proper moral sensitivity by feeling grateful, providing of course that the motive was indeed that of intending to help.

On the other hand a case can be made that some people do indeed have a moral obligation to help those in need, even if it is only an imperfect duty. Does the temporary part-time laborer who now narrowly escapes starvation but still lives in poverty have a moral duty to help people like the homeless woman who is even worse off than he is? He has no such obligation if some minimal security level should hold before any such moral obligation can be considered reasonable. His financial situation, after all, is anything but secure or promising. But for the rich man, things are very different. A number of influential contemporary social philosophers and theorists from a range of backgrounds and approaches argue that the affluent have a far more compelling duty to help those in dire need than libertarians realize.[8] Some go further and argue for a stronger obligation than that of an imperfect duty. Peter Singer, for example, ruffles a lot of feathers when he appeals to classical utilitarianism to argue that not only is there an obligation to relieve those suffering in poverty, but that the obligation is far more stringent than most people think. His papers, "Famine, Affluence, and Morality" and "Rich and Poor," startled many readers, the more so since he clearly does not relegate this obligation solely to institutions like governments.[9] Sometimes this claimed obligation on the part of the affluent has been explicitly addressed in the recent work on gratitude.

Lyons clearly sympathizes with the notion that there is some kind of moral obligation for the wealthy to help the poor. He writes that

> the poor have a human right to be helped by being shared-with (under the modest assumption that a redistributed dollar will help the poor man more than its loss will cost the rich man). And my suggestion would be that for this sharing the poor owe the rich only perfunctory thanks [i.e., not "real thanks"], if any.[10]

The question of whether the wealthy have strict moral obligations to help those in need is not one I can investigate here, but it serves well to illustrate how the G/NO principle functions: if the wealthy have such an obligation, no "real" thanks and no gratitude is "owed." I will examine this connection more closely (i.e., being grateful only for help that is not morally owed), since however plausible, I believe it is unsound.

I will also look at the approach itself that is usually taken in applying the principle to actual situations, since that too involves a concern I have with this standard position. It's a problem of a basic kind: much of traditional philosophy conceives of moral action as occurring between free-standing individuals, paradigmatically just two. That is to say, an adequate portrayal of the situation consists of describing the relevant actions, attitudes, motives, and attributes of those two individuals and nothing more. The relevant facts about them may vary from one case to another, ranging from pieces of behavior to thoughts and even feelings, but only those two people are involved. In the case of the passerby giving money to the destitute homeless person, there are two key players: the one giving the money and the one receiving it.

This way of morally assessing a situation or an interaction, so often found in both moral theory and political philosophy, has come under repeated attack in more recent years, especially from feminist moral and political philosophers. It distorts the findings on so many issues and does so here, when examining gratitude. Most of the literature on gratitude that follows shortly on Lyons' article makes no attempt to embed the interaction between the benefactor and the recipient in the prevailing social structures, to note the web of relationships in which the two people are actually living, to explore any systematic difference in power that may hold between benefactor and recipient, and to reflect on the relevance of these factors. It is all much simpler than this. The main requirements for gratitude are that one individual helps another (in a way that is not morally obligatory) and the motive passes muster. If gratitude is not in order, then either the help was indeed morally owed or it is because of something directly to do with one of those two people, like the helper having a murky motive.

It's probably no accident that this way of approaching a moral analysis of some everyday situation has historically been accompanied by the ideal of an individual as "independent," someone who can choose to form relationships or not, someone who savors his personal "liberty" and charts his own course. An individual at his best does not allow himself to be tied to others in ways that threaten or limit his freedom, his autonomy. In the memorable characterization given by Margaret Urban Walker in her book, *Moral Understandings*,

> "Autonomous man," that...protagonist of modern moral philosophy...is disembodied, disembedded, unencumbered, affectless, isolated, detached, unpleasantly self-interested, defensively self-protective, abnormally self-reliant, and narcissistically self-reflective.[11]

This characterization, of course, contains within itself the touch-points for feminist critique. The ideal of an individual free of significant entanglements with others, forging his own way forward, focused heavily on his own future and well-being whether or not that be at the expense of others, adds up to a toxic brew.

Even if we temporarily set aside the now familiar criticisms of this as a kind of "ideal" person, the basic idea of thinking of individuals as simply unconnected to others is in itself misleading. Elizabeth Wolgast refers to this as the "social atomism" approach to moral issues where society is seen as "a simple collection of independent, self-motivated units."[12] It is "made up of individual people, as bricks in a wall, as molecules in a substance"; they are "complete and real, each in him- or herself."[13] Or again, as Iris Marion Young notes, with this model, individuals are conceived as "social atoms, logically prior to social relations and institutions."[14] If we see individuals in this way, then it's not surprising that we analyze moral situations by looking only at actions, intentions, perhaps thoughts and feelings, of just the individuals directly involved in the situation. It is an approach that overlooks the social structures that may play a key role and that may make a moral difference.

It is not a sound way to determine the proper moral response to help received. Returning to our paradigm case of someone giving food or money to someone in great need, let us assume for the sake of argument that the very poor have no obligation to help someone marginally worse off than they are, but that the wealthy do have a duty to help those in great need, especially when it will not significantly affect their own comfort and well-being. Should we expect the recipient to feel gratitude toward either benefactor, given that ex hypothesi the motive for both men, the rich man and the temporary laborer, is to help?

The G/NO connection is of course to do with a necessary, not a sufficient, condition for gratitude's being a proper response. Even so, the fact that most of the literature so far referred to systematically omits any condition that is not tied to the key players as individuals conveys a tacit message: that all we need to know in order to decide if gratitude is appropriate are features of the individuals directly involved and whether or not the action was morally obligatory. The message is not logically entailed, but rather contextually conveyed. Given that we are assuming for the sake of argument that the temporary laborer (who is very poor) has no obligation to help the homeless woman and that the rich man does, then it seems that gratitude is a fitting response to the laborer, but not to the wealthy man. As sensible as these two claims seem, I think they oversimplify what's involved. We need to take account of more of the moral situation.

With respect to the poor benefactor, a fairly straightforward point illustrates why the usually cited necessary conditions taken together do not constitute a sufficient condition for gratitude being appropriate. This does not literally conflict with the G/NO principle, but it does draw attention to the selectively limited focus of the principle and it does alert us to the dangers of an overly "atomistic" approach that considers only the individuals directly involved in the incident.

The case of the rich benefactor more directly challenges the G/NO connection.

I will argue that gratitude may not be fitting for reasons other than the G/N principle.

More controversially *I believe there are cases where gratitude is appropriate in the case of the wealthy helper even if we assume that he has a moral obligation to give aid.* If these points are correct, then the G/NO connection itself oversimplifies the moral story and this has implications for situations of civilized oppression.

The Moral Relevance of Relationships

Each individual is embedded in a network of relationships, some more personal and intimate, others much less so. These relationships involve time, energy, decisions, rewarding experiences, harms, and blows to the self-esteem. They often involve emotional output, public support, public humiliation, interesting interactions and futile exchanges, and much more. Life is lived in relationships. And to a large degree they are socially structured. There are systematic power differences involved, differences that cannot be understood simply by looking at dyadic relationships between supposedly "free-standing" individuals. Sometimes there are forms of power at work involving unseen third parties and these kinds of power have profound effects on how someone develops as a person and interacts with various others, and even on how she perceives herself.[15]

How can the relationships surrounding the benefactor, the agent, affect the moral status of gratitude? Beginning with the temporary laborer, surely the man who has just earned a tiny bit of money not immediately needed for food and shelter deserves gratitude if he gives any of it to the person in even greater need? He wants to help, even if his help is inevitably very limited. Of course in doing so he is taking a risk, since he has no backup funds if he suddenly loses the part-time job as a laborer, but surely it is his right to take that risk?

But there are possibilities that could make a difference. If he has young children who are entirely dependent on him, then even if they have barely adequate food as things are, they (not only he himself) are put more at risk by this giving. If he has no supportive intimates or friends in his life and (ex hypothesi) no government-provided safety net, then increasing the risk to such vulnerable dependents may be morally irresponsible. They are even more vulnerable than the homeless woman and he has a special responsibility for their safety and welfare. Is gratitude a fitting response to the help in such circumstances, even if his motive was indeed to help? The point is that *to say gratitude is appropriate is, among other things, to endorse the basic moral status of the action*, the giving of help, and just as a person's responsibility, freedom, options, and so on cannot be seen by looking solely at the individual, so too the moral status of an action cannot be well assessed by maintaining a tunnel vision on that particular, directly visible action and those directly and most immediately affected by it. If the beneficiary welcomes the help and knows nothing beyond the immediate situation, she may well be grateful and the attitude involves nothing morally dubious on her part. But if on the other hand she happens to know the whole story, it's a fair question whether or not she should welcome the help in the sense of morally endorsing the action, even though her situation is serious. Our example involves what are usually called special relationships and if they at least sometimes take precedence over regard for strangers, then such relationships can have a direct bearing on when gratitude is appropriate. More than this, one could easily make the case that yet more urgent obligations to other strangers could take precedence over helping the woman in need. It is not enough to note that the benefactor's motive is to help the recipient when there is no moral duty to help, and that this help is welcomed and appreciated by the recipient. We need to look beyond the dyadic interaction and the presence or absence of the most obvious form of moral obligation between the benefactor and the one helped. We need to reflect on more than this before concluding that gratitude is appropriate. This illustrative example, though, ultimately still points to individuals, even though they (the children) are not present at the scene.

More interesting is the case of the rich benefactor. The prevailing view is that even though his motive is what it should be, gratitude is not fitting since he has a moral obligation to help those in great need. The G/NO principle is what determines the answer in these circumstances since it points to a necessary condition, which is lacking in this case. But even if we assume for the moment that this G/NO principle is correct (and I do not think it is), we are missing important parts of the moral story if we cite as the crucial reason for our answer that the agent has a moral duty to help (and helping is his motive).

What else may be relevant? Even considering only the economic issues, suppose that nearly all of the wealthy elite in that society have accumulated their riches by a system designed to "get the most out of" those who have to work to live. They close down factories without notice, move factories to locations where welfare and worker safety are nonissues if this increases profits, and they seek to replace workers with technology, again, in order to raise profits, sporadically leaving thousands with no secure access to even the most minimal basic needs. If they have not been personally and directly involved in this system, they have at least inherited their wealth from those who have.

Let us further suppose that the rich benefactor belongs to such a family and is privileged in many ways, most of which he is unaware of. His sense of self is shaped by the day-to-day security and luxury he takes for granted, the power and influence he habitually exercises, the freedom from tedious and dangerous labor that his money provides, the deference typically shown to him, and his views by those less advantageously placed (especially those in poverty). He never reflects on his privilege and security. He has no first-hand experience of poverty, hunger, powerlessness, or marginalization, has never seriously engaged with those who have, and has no interest in learning about their life-situations. When confronted by the actual sight of the woman in such dire straits, he is genuinely distressed and gives her money, but makes no mental connection between her plight and his own ongoing business practices or family involvement. There is, in fact, no sense of involvement or accountability. His self-image is that of a disinterested passerby who is moved by compassion to act benevolently.

These things, I contend, make a difference to a moral assessment of the situation. If the network of relationships in which he lives, the power and privilege he daily enjoys, mold him in this way, then even though he is trying to help the person he sees, a lot is going wrong here. And if gratitude is set aside solely on the grounds that he has an obligation to help, then we do not reach these matters and are unlikely to reflect on their significance. That is to say, even if we suppose for the moment that there is no obligation at all to help, or that helping those in dire need is an imperfect duty and so there is no obligation for him to help in this particular case, there is still too much wrong, too much tainting of the relationship for gratitude to be appropriate, even though the motive was genuinely to help.

Gratitude after all is an attitude directed to the benefactor rather than simply to the benefit. Fred Berger writes that "When we show gratitude [it is the] display of the other's attitude towards us to which we are responding."[16] So far so good. But he clarifies this by saying that "If I am the recipient of another's benevolence, his action indicates he cares about me, he values me, he respects me."[17] This generalization, however, is insecure if it is based on too atomistic an approach to the occasions of benevolence. Looking at the dyadic interaction is not an adequate basis for such a general claim and in particular the benefactor's respect for the recipient is not established so easily. Respect may require compassion, but there is far more to it than that. The rich man may well be distressed by the painful need of the woman he helps, but if there is a willful refusal to think about his own role in there being so many like her who live in poverty, if he never has the time or the interest to learn more about what it is like to live without adequate resources, if he never thinks about how their situation might be improved in a more ongoing fashion, then his respect for the poor in his society, including the woman he sees, is considerably below what it should be and isolated acts of benevolence cannot undo this.

As already noted, saying that gratitude is appropriate involves among other things morally endorsing the action. To this I will now add that it also *requires us to morally endorse some basic aspects of the relationship involved*. It does not require a perfect or ideal relationship, whatever that would look like, but if we believe that basic human relations should embody mutual respect, then some reasonable level of respect should exist in the relationship between helper and recipient. What such respect involves can increase in the case of relationships between intimates and friends, but even in the case of strangers, even unseen strangers, there are clear instances where basic respect is lacking and I think the rich man in our hypothesized example is such a case even if he is unaware of his attitude.

Setting aside the G/NO connection, then, there are other, often unmentioned, concerns that affect whether gratitude is a proper response. They are usefully distinguished from the G/NO doctrine since they are more to do with the *nature of the relationship* than with *the morally obligatory nature or otherwise of the action*, and they form an important part of the moral account of gratitude.

The recipient of course may not know all the relevant facts and may still be grateful even if they are known, but this empirical fact would not threaten the moral account I am giving here. In our example the woman who receives the bit of money is herself embedded in a set of socially structured relationships where things are stacked up against her. Let us say that she is without means, without meaningful employment. She is a woman, a woman of color, not well educated, not verbally articulate, and not "good looking" by society's stereotypes. She is excluded from influential public activities and organizations. No one seeks her views or even listens if she gives them. She is trained into silence. She is largely invisible except as a nuisance and is acutely aware of being powerless both with respect to the future direction of her own life and those of the people closest to her. Let us add that in this instance, as in so many like it, her self-esteem or lack of it has been shaped by these facts. Even worse, her self-respect has eroded over the years. At one time she used to reflect now and again on how others treated her, all too often with the same depressing conclusion: that others who were in a better social position behaved toward her with systematic disrespect. Out of a kind of self-protection, she no longer reflects on the deeper aspects of others' behavior toward her and her spirits have sunk to the point where she no longer cares whether others treat her with respect. She is grateful for the money the affluent give her, but however understandable, this in itself does not show that gratitude is well placed.

If we think that the rich man does have an obligation to help in this instance, then on the G/NO principle, this is sufficient to make gratitude inappropriate. It functions rather like a trump card here and it masks moral issues to do with the nature of the underlying relationship. If we suppose that the rich benefactor has no obligation to help the woman in need, whether in this specific situation (which is compatible with an imperfect duty to help those in need) or in some more general, across the board fashion, then we see past the principle not only to the action of helping, but to the nature of the relationship between them. A morally distorted relationship can taint the whole transaction, even though help (money) was given. If the rich benefactor lacks genuine and nonsuperficial respect for the woman, then even if there is no obligation to help, a case can be made for gratitude being misplaced. It is humiliating to be expected to be grateful for a bit of help from a member of the group whose greed, callousness, and willful ignorance play key roles in the situation of dire need one is in. At least, it ought to be humiliating if one's self-respect has not already been eroded.

Feminists and a Non-Atomistic Approach

Although it is still not unusual in moral philosophy for the approach to be atomistic (as this term has been explained), more recent work by feminist philosophers and others working on oppression have emphasized the formative role of socially structured relationships on matters like autonomy, civil liberty, opportunities, self-esteem, self-respect, and more. One of the refreshing aspects of Claudia Card's article, "Gratitude and Obligation," is the keen awareness of various kinds of socially constructed power differences.[18] The problematic atomism that plagues so much of the work is absent. Card reaches past the visible individual and clearly distinguishes the socially powerful from the powerless. For example:

> Historically, the powerful and privileged have imposed *their* guardianship upon the powerless and have felt the latter should be grateful for their "care."[19]

Again:

> When the powerful are generous, it may be simply that they enjoy giving. It supports their own self-esteem; it demonstrates their wealth and power. Such generosity can be accompanied by insensitivity to others wishes' [*sic*] with regard to becoming obligated. The powerful can afford not to care whether others are obligated or not.

> Gratitude regarding such a benefactor need not be misplaced. One may be grateful *that* the benefactor is there without being grateful *to* anyone. To think one *owes* the benefactor, however, may be either to misjudge the latter or to fail to respect oneself.[20]

The disadvantaged person being helped may be grateful *that* the socially privileged person is there to give help, but need not be grateful *to* the socially powerful benefactor. In fact, it seems to be suggested that she should not be.

In a number of ways I am sympathetic to this. To begin with, it's interesting that instead of simply applying the G/NO principle to these situations, Card looks past this trump card and notes things to do with the attitudes of the privileged toward the disadvantaged, their display of power, and their involvement of the privileged in the plight of those in dire need. As Card claims, "It can be argued that [the privileged] have often been responsible for the neediness of the powerless, that their attempts to obligate the latter by meeting those needs is a racket."[21]

This brings me to a second matter, Card's characterization of the wealthy and powerful, which leads me to the second main point in this chapter. The G/NO principle at the center of the standard position I've been considering insists, of course, that if there is an obligation to help, then this in itself is enough to make any gratitude misplaced. Whether or not the wealthy benefactor does have an obligation to help in the sample case is not settled here, but I wish now to move to what is probably the most controversial claim, namely, that gratitude is sometimes appropriate even if the helper has a moral obligation to give aid. This claim challenges the G/NO principle directly.

Civilized Oppression and the G/NO Principle

There is nothing technically incorrect in Card's characterization of the wealthy and the otherwise socially privileged. She claims that the affluent *may* give because they enjoy giving, because it boosts their self-esteem and shows off their social status. This *can* be accompanied by an insensitivity to the wishes of those being helped. And indeed these things may often be the case. It was not difficult earlier in the chapter to describe the particular rich man of our example as self-centered, habitually exploitative, and willfully unaware.

But there is a danger in overgeneralizing, in coming close to a blanket stereotype of the privileged. We have only one picture of the privileged helper as someone who, aware of the fact or not, relishes the power it brings, can help the less advantaged without sacrifices, and welcomes or at least does nothing to discourage the sense of obligation the subordinated beneficiaries acquire. Card writes that "The powerful, at any rate, have no general interest in rejecting the [powerless recipients'] gratitude or discouraging their sense of obligation."[22] The tacit thought seems to be that if it is not in their interest, it will not happen.

How is this overgeneralized? Is it not true that those who have always had multiple forms of socially constructed power tend to be unaware of it, call upon it habitually, and develop a level of self-esteem that has a lot to do with social success, the sense of control over one's life, and the deference and appreciation so often received? Yes, often, perhaps still predominantly, but there remain also self-reflective individuals who think about day-to-day incidents, listen to the perceptions of the less powerful, and begin to have doubts about common social practices and some of their own usual ways of dealing with others.

Suppose that our rich helper is not the willfully unreflective benefactor mentioned earlier, but rather someone with a morally inquiring nature who asks questions and engages in discussions that are unpopular with most of his social peers, someone who has a sincere interest in the lives of others and worries about major and persistent social differences that seem unrelated to personal "desert" or widespread well-being.

It is true that one of the points emphasized in this book is that distortions occur in our moral analyses if an atomistic approach to morality is a guiding principle. But equally, problems arise if there is no recognition of individual differences, particularly with respect to moral character and particularly if the individual belongs to a group whose interests are better served by a close-minded and unthinking approach to life. The moral danger of stereotypes is as high here as in other contexts that feminist philosophers have analyzed. It is as high here as it is in the case of stereotyping the victims of civilized oppression.

This matters when thinking about gratitude when we remember what such a person may do. The person's actions may be aimed not simply at helping an individual in need, one whose difficulties visibly present themselves, but rather aimed at some aspect of the power structure or social mechanism that lies behind her disadvantaged state. Some of the "help" may take a form that recognizes the systematic nature of the deprivation, perhaps by taking part in a campaign to raise funds for literacy programs or donating time at a free medical clinic. More significantly for my purposes, he may target oppressive power structures more directly by publicly arguing for an adequate minimum wage or by resigning from the "men only" social club.

It will be objected that he is simply doing what he should do and indeed should not have joined the exclusive club in the first place. All this may be true, although awareness of the nonviolently immoral in things that are very familiar is difficult for everyone, both the privileged and the oppressed. What is different here from the earlier benefactor is that the person is knowingly and intentionally breaking ranks with his social peers and this is not a trivial matter.

We are typically exhorted to nurture gratitude for help that is risky or very costly for the helper. Gratitude toward the person who runs into the burning building and saves me is well-directed since, on most accounts at least, the action is morally supererogatory. Risking life itself is clearly a very high risk. It is easy to admire risk-taking when the possible costs involve material changes of a dramatic kind, like loss of life, health, home, family, job, or financial security. With such material changes, the bar can be set high enough to move the status of the action from obligatory to supererogatory, and so gratitude is appropriate. Recognition for sacrifices is harder to achieve when the costs involve less tangible, less material kinds of matters.

Yet, just as the harms and wrongs experienced by the victims of nonviolent oppression are serious but subtle, so too are the risks and costs experienced by some of the powerful who meet certain obligations. Often the harm and denigration experienced by victims of civilized oppression take forms that are anything but highly visible to bystanders or to agents who are not affected. It all seems so trivial. Yet in recent decades, feminist writers and also writers concerned with other common forms of (here, nonviolent) oppression have articulated the true nature of the victims' experiences and their ongoing and cumulative impact. Yet more than the oppressive agents' actions and more than the victims' experiences are involved here. I have argued in earlier work that the nature of the relationships in which someone is embedded lies at the heart of nonviolent oppression and that the sense of being excluded, ignored, scorned, and even blamed contributes heavily to an oppressed life-situation. The relationships themselves as distinct from the various forms of material deprivation associated with them carry a heavy load in such oppression, the more so since the harms and wrongs they involve are far from trivial and yet hard to perceive.[23]

But just as those not affected often do not perceive the harm and moral subordination that is the lot of victims of civilized oppression, so too it is quite possible for those victims to miss and/or seriously belittle the costs paid by the privileged who break ranks, who display a lamentable lack of solidarity with and loyalty to the relevant group. As their numbers grow, the significance of the costs can be expected to lessen; they will be breaking ranks with fewer and fewer of their peers. But that time is quite a long way away. The deeply felt attitudes and perceptions of the socially advantaged cannot literally be coerced and they will in practice be revealed even if those involved are maneuvered into following laws and institutional regulations (and it should be said in passing that achieving such compliance is far more difficult in fact than many realize). An otherwise socially powerful individual can pay a higher price than most observers realize for acts that challenge or condemn the existing social structures. There may be no material losses of any significant kind, but there are other kinds of costs and they involve the kind of harms and misery the oppressed are all too familiar with. The person's views are no longer warmly received by many of his social peers and deference is no longer given. He is interrupted more, treated dismissively, no longer invited to join in the activities of the group, and no longer kept informed about important matters. He is often seen as naive and an embarrassment to the group; the "old guard" will predictably disassociate themselves from him. Those close to him, perhaps in special relationships with him, may be condemned by association and he must watch the effects of any such fallout on them, knowing that his actions and attitudes are causally responsible for it. The relationship network in which he is socially located is transformed and he is marginalized or excluded outright.

Furthermore, unlike the oppressed who have harms and belittlement imposed upon them, the privileged who breaks ranks has it within his control to prevent or reverse the process, at least in its early stages. A simple loyalty to the group is expected and defections are often penalized. There is an obvious temptation to "keep one's head down" and "mind one's own business," all the stronger, since such silence and noninvolvement will not only prevent these subtle harms, it will be actively rewarded. The temptation to comply, to be loyal to the traditional stance, is strong;

the temptation to reverse early moves into a moral and intellectual independence which, he finds, is both scorned and penalized is even stronger. It takes some moral courage to show solidarity with the oppressed, since this begins to realign the relationships between the oppressed and the agents of their oppression. And by its very nature, breaking ranks is a lonely business. The likely outcome is isolation from his social peers.

And what is the likely outcome with respect to the relationship between himself and the victims of civilized oppression? He may indeed be recognized for what he is and what he is doing. In practice, though, the danger of stereotypes and overgeneralizations is high and victims who do not know him personally or even in the longer term may well continue to distrust and condemn him as a member of the oppressive group. And like all of us, he will not be infallible in his judgment; he will make mistakes no matter how sound his motives. For those predisposed to mistrust, there will inevitably be situations and opportunities to (incorrectly) impugn his character or his true intentions when such a mistake occurs. It is not a small thing to receive forms of hostility from those for whom risks were taken, sacrifices made, and costs incurred. It is painful, and again constitutes an ongoing temptation to fall back into line and leave the isolation of being unwelcome and unvalued by many from both the group of peers and the group of victims.

Also the privileged who adopt attitudes and perform actions counter to the oppressive habits of their socially powerful group typically grew up with those habits or at least saw them as commonplace within their families or close circle of acquaintances. This in fact is part of what is involved in being a member of that group early on in the stages of reform. Often those who break away have made personal changes as a result of their increasing awareness of the connections between these habits and civilized oppression. Yet to live life reflectively means facing those occasions when we come to realize that past actions were morally wrong, sometimes systematically so. Growing awareness and moral insight do not simply make for an exciting adventure. They bring with them the pain of failure, especially with respect to the past, even if there was no awareness of the immorality at the time. The textbook distinction between action and agent may change the nature of the pain but rarely succeeds in removing it. That is to say, such a reflective person feels badly about morally unacceptable actions performed in the past, even if they were performed without awareness of their moral status. It takes courage to live a life of moral endeavor and the privileged agent loses the self-deceptive peace of mind that so often accompanies willful ignorance. A moral approach often calls for uncomfortable commitments.

So, even though they are doing what morally they should, I think that for the reasons explained above, gratitude for such break-away "heroes" need not be misplaced. The risks and costs involved can and often are a lot more significant than meets the eye in the same way as the costs that are the lot of the victims of civilized oppression. They are costs more often than not unrecognized and belittled if perceived at all. The victims of civilized oppression can miss their significance in the same way as many miss the costs paid by the victims of such oppression, so there is typically no appreciation of what being a break-away member of the privileged group can require. The situation is especially demanding morally, in that the person usually has the power to move back into compliance with the group and that there can be a temptation to do so is obvious. It therefore demands a degree of self-discipline that is not only high, but has the capacity to make the person feel like a fool for following what moral obligation dictates in the fact of widespread rejection, even by the victims on whose behalf the risks are taken and the costs paid. The person is aware that stereotypes and overgeneralizations will, in very many cases, lead to hasty and unpleasant judgments about him by the oppressed victims. He also knows that inevitably he will occasionally make an error of judgment and so, very probably, also an mistaken decision about some action, and that this will even more surely result in his being categorized as one of the uncaring, arrogant, willfully unaware oppressors by victims who do not know him well. And if, as is true of many, he himself has made personal changes in order to tackle his oppressive socialized habits, then he must live with the knowledge that prior to those insights, he was himself an agent of oppression. He is, I believe, doing what is morally called for, but I equally believe that what he does is anything but easy or trivial, especially where there are still few of the powerful group who actually do perceive the range of moral wrong civilized oppression involves.

So I conclude that we can sometimes properly be grateful to someone who has done what morally ought to be done, and in that case the G/ NO principle is faulty.

Gratitude and the Limitations of Thinking of "Help"

The main body of recent literature on gratitude is misleading in another way also, since it is not just help in the ordinary sense of the word that properly elicits gratitude. Claudia Card is atypical in that she includes in the occasions for gratitude quite a range of events, like receiving "a gift, a favor, a rescue, support and encouragement, recognition, sympathy, any number of things people do for me or give me beyond what they owed me."[24] But could they all be subsumed under the umbrella term of "help"? Perhaps at a pinch, but it is quite a pinch. Normally we speak of help when what is given or done makes some kind of practical difference to the recipient. The gift certificate enables her to buy new hockey gear. The rescue from being lost in the woods means she is spared frostbite the cold night would have caused. The encouragement boosts her spirits and she tries again to study for the exam. The help makes a practical differ-ence, whether it be to the material situation or to the person's psychologi-cal state or feelings. There is *some* expectation along those lines, which is why we sometimes hear things like, "Kate came over and talked with me. In fact she said all kinds of encouraging things. She meant well, I know, and I didn't feel up to telling her that it didn't help. It made no difference. I still can't study for the exam."

Perhaps a piece of tidying up is all that is needed. Given the right motives, gratitude is a proper response to someone's helping me or at least trying to. I suggest, however, that this is too narrow an account. In par-ticular, if we again set aside an overly atomistic approach and take note of the social structures, then I can identify myself as a member of this and that group and I can be properly grateful for actions that protest futilely on behalf of that group, or acts that bestow recognition on that group, or acts that involve listening to members of the group, and so on, even if those acts are not directed toward me personally and even if it is crystal clear that those acts cannot in fact make any practical difference to either my own situation or the situation of the group as a whole.

Why is gratitude appropriate in such cases? There may be some desirable consequences that would follow if gratitude is felt and expressed. (Perhaps gratitude will encourage further subversive activities on their part, for example.) But such a flat-footed account does not get to the heart of the matter. There do not have to be desirable consequences for some act to signify such recognition or respect or moral solidarity. We have more to be grateful for than help in the straightforward sense. Respect for our moral status, even when those who are signaling respect cannot help, deserves gratitude. In fact, it deserves gratitude even if those respected never hear about it, never know about it, and if those who disrespect them make no desirable changes. It *deserves* respect even if ex hypothesi the respected, now knowing about the situation, cannot feel or express it.

Gratitude in fact involves more than individuals doing certain kinds of things. It is part of bringing to life the notion of a moral community. This conception of community need not of course refer to a collection of isolated individuals all striving to live as independently of each other as possible, all focused first and foremost on their own self-interests. It is a vision of relatedness, empathy, mutual protection of the vulnerable, affirmation, interaction, a sense of belonging, and more, even when the people are for the most part technically strangers.

Is Gratitude Demeaning?

I am not here developing the notion of a moral community. Rather I am pointing to a connection between gratitude and the notion of community. The notion is relevant to how we should see ourselves when we are the recipients of help or some act of moral solidarity. Traditionally there has been some strong resistance to accepting aid. Kant, for example, voices a very angst-ridden view on this. He writes that,

> If I accept favours, I contract debts which I can never repay, for I can never get on equal terms with him who has conferred the favours upon me; he has stolen a march upon me, and if I do him a favour I am only returning a quid pro quo; I shall always owe him a debt of gratitude, and who will accept such a debt?[25]

How bad can it be? Says Kant,

> To be indebted is to be subject to an unending constraint. I must forever be courteous and flattering towards my benefactor, and if I fail to be so he will very soon make me conscious of my failure; I may even be forced to use subterfuge so as to avoid meeting him. But he who pays promptly for everything is under no constraint; he is free to act as he please; none will hinder him.[26]

This paints a grim picture of gratitude (although it's hard not to smile at the thought of Kant crossing the street and dashing into doorways in order to avoid meeting his "benefactor"). The "debt of gratitude" is intolerably burdensome because it can never be paid off, and it is also demeaning because I am now constrained in my behavior toward my benefactor, even to the point of becoming sycophantic. It is perhaps ironic that Kant finds it so distasteful to accept help, given how much emphasis he places on respect. But then, much depends on how one construes respect and how one envisions the moral community.

In my view, helping each other, especially the more vulnerable, is part of what "community" stands far. Not all pieces of "help" by the more privileged to the disadvantaged are given in the right moral spirit of genuine respect, but some do embody the basic human endeavor to be more morally alert and committed and also to be supportive of others. Perhaps the conception of a far from impersonal moral community requires both the socially elite and the disadvantaged to conceive of a kind of connectedness, so that support, empathy, and help is naturally given, accepted, and shared without ulterior motives and without embarrassment. (It is as vital for this conception that accepting help is seen as a natural part of community, just as much as giving help is.) A rich conception of moral community can serve both to underpin the appropriateness of gratitude and also to challenge the view that the position of gratitude is inherently demeaning. There need be nothing humiliating about being grateful, even if the gratitude is properly directed to a far more powerful and privileged person. Such a community is an ideal to work toward and the pathway may differ for differently situated individuals. And it is why, other things being equal, we should be able to accept nonpaternalistic help without feeling indebted and why we should be able to feel and show gratitude without feeling demeaned. It is a vision of building relationships that undermine those embedded in oppressive social structures, new relationships, where among other things self-respect is secure and nonpaternalistic help is just one of many usual acts of inclusion and mutual respect. In such a community, being appropriately grateful is not inherently demeaning.

CHAPTER 3

The Relationship of Moral Solidarity

In this chapter I explore a morally rich notion of solidarity and the relationships it promotes, and in doing so, argue for the role of empathetic understanding in the moral response to civilized oppression. This is a position generally accepted in feminist philosophy, but I introduce two caveats that extend the role of moral solidarity in controversial ways.

There is currently no agreed upon meaning given to "moral solidarity," so I explore the question: how should we conceive of moral solidarity if we are to reach a morally rich conception of that bond, something morally worth striving for? After rejecting two apparently plausible candidates, I examine the relationship between members of an oppressed group and relatively powerful, non-oppressed others to see what can this suggest about a desirable form of moral solidarity.

The vocabulary of oppression has steadily grown as vulnerable groups at the receiving end of the injustice have come to be identified: classism, racism, sexism, heterosexism or homophobia, ageism, ableism, and more. The systematic nature of what is wrong is an essential feature of oppression and typically victims lack effective power with which to stop it. The power difference between the perpetrators and victims is one reason why references to "solidarity" are increasingly heard. Morally speaking, others need to be involved in these situations. If there was less oppression in the world, we would hear far less about solidarity.

Studying the current literature, however, there seems to be no agreed upon meaning of the term solidarity, nor even a clear consensus as to the kind of item it refers to. Is it an action, a motive, an attitude, a piece of political activism, or something else? Even without complete consensus, perhaps there are still a few common threads. First, solidarity involves at least two individuals or two groups: one is in solidarity with another. Second, we are in solidarity with those suffering from immorality or injustice, not from some natural disaster. Third, action may be involved, but there seems at least to be agreement that action alone is not enough. No matter what the action, if it is self-serving (e.g., a matter of career advancement or impressing family and friends or winning an award), solidarity is not an appropriate term to use. There is some kind of alignment or unity or fellowship involved, although the nature of it is a matter of debate.

It may be some years before there is enough consensus in the literature to speak about "correct" and "incorrect" uses of the word, but I think we can move in on some of the interesting moral issues even so. We can ask if, on some plausible reading of solidarity, it could refer to something morally sound, possibly morally called for, and if so, what this would be like and why it would be morally desirable, especially in situations of civilized oppression (given the focus of the work).

Solidarity involves a bond, but what kind of bond is it? Or to phrase it in a more approachable fashion, how should we conceive of the bond if we are to reach a morally rich conception of solidarity, something morally worth striving for? I will here develop a position mentioned briefly in the book, *Civilized Oppression*.[1] In this earlier work, I argue that the more powerful typically have a moral obligation to be in moral solidarity with the oppressed, and that while acts of solidarity (e.g., acts of protest) are clearly morally important, I maintain that such acts are conceived of as reflections of a *relationship of solidarity*. The relationship itself is morally more foundational here than the acts and involves more than just acts. Since there is not yet a settled, "correct" meaning of solidarity, I am seeking a plausible reading of moral solidarity that captures something morally desirable, a reason for its desirability, and one or two interesting implications of the position.

Are Shared Goals Not Enough?

I begin with what is perhaps the simplest context for considering solidarity: the potential solidarity between victims of oppression. Even without any details, it may seem that a simple approach will suffice. After all, does it not make sense to speak of solidarity if two individuals or groups act together in pursuit of a common goal, if they combine their resources to achieve something they are both aiming for? Connections are indeed often formed when two different groups have some shared goals, but this does not ensure any sweeping compatibility of aims. For example, victims of oppression may be physically attacked, terrorized, actively exploited, ignored, scorned, or excluded, and the priorities for different oppressed groups may vary at any one time. If two groups unite because they are working toward some shared goal, I will speak of "an alliance." Such a connection can be made for fairly specific practical aims that assist both groups and it may continue for a shorter or longer time. Yet although there may be mutual practical support with respect to the goals, it is not clear that anything more need be involved. An alliance in a common cause does not even ensure good feelings between the two groups in any general sense. Such mutual support can be very practically oriented and have quite stringent boundaries placed on it. In fact when the goals are achieved, there may be a parting of ways. This is especially likely if the alliance is in order to work against some anticipated event, which, when dealt with, leaves the two groups reverting to their own agendas, which may well conflict in some respects.

In World War II the alliance between Russia and the Allies against Nazi Germany and other Axis powers was predictably short-lived. The longer-term goals of the two parties were far too much in conflict for anything more. "Uniting against a common enemy" can be a practical tactic for groups with otherwise very disparate aims and commitments. If the shared aims are few and specific, then no matter how long the joint endeavor lasts, there seems to be too little by way of "unity" for this to count as solidarity. The rhetoric of solidarity and other emotively laden language may indeed be used in such situations as a way of artificially boosting the image of the kind of connection made. Even practical alliances are difficult to get off the ground if one party announces at the start that as soon as the main shared goal is achieved, the next goal will be to attack or incapacitate the temporary "ally." The illusion of something more may allow the limited connection to function successfully in the shorter term. Such glosses, though, rarely deceive for long, and history, with clearer hindsight, usually gives a more honest account. An alliance need not be as restricted as this, but if it reasonably can be, an alliance in itself cannot be counted on to involve solidarity. Something more is surely involved, or rather, more should be involved if solidarity is to be something morally desirable in itself and not simply practically useful. Could an alliance be described as "political solidarity" or "activist solidarity"? Other writers are better positioned to debate the merits of this, but if such labels are to be used for such connections, then I should state clearly that what I am exploring is something different, something that, among other things, very much involves the individuals as individuals, best captured as moral solidarity.

The "Something More" and Comembership in an Oppressed Group

Can this something more be counted on when speaking of comembers of an oppressed group, victims suffering from the same form of oppression? The question itself requires caution since an oppressed individual can of course be a member of more than one oppressed group. A woman of color living in poverty in an affluent society will encounter more than one kind of prejudice and be vulnerable in more than one respect. Her life-situation and experiences will differ from those of a rich woman of color living in the same society (although it is not as simple as "adding or subtracting" a prejudice).[2]

But suppose we have a group of people whose situation seems to be more homogeneous than this and who do seem to agree on some important shared goals in their struggle against their subordination. Does this ensure something more than a practical alliance in the sense described above?

Perhaps the benefit most to be expected in this situation is shared knowledge of the injustices involved in such oppression. Given a reasonable level of self-awareness, comembers of the group will probably know about and recognize the kinds of unfairness associated with membership in the group. As Laurence Thomas remarks in his article, "Moral Flourishing in an Unjust World," "persons belonging to the same diminished social category [the same oppressed group] may have breathtaking insight into the experiences of one another."[3] Such shared knowledge is an advantage in setting appropriate goals and one might expect the united action of the group to be more effective.

Yet all this is compatible with a generally selfish approach on the part of individual group members. Bob knows the kinds of snubs, insults, and name-calling he and others on social assistance experience in their daily lives. He talks with others in the same situation, he encourages cooperation and joint action, but only because he knows that this is the only way his own situation may be improved; nothing can be gained if he acts alone. Suppose the provincial government stipulates that recipients of "welfare checks" must line up outside a designated office at a specific morning and time in order to receive them. Checks will no longer be mailed out, not even to those with a stable address (and this actually occurred in one Canadian province). In larger cities, queues of several hundred recipients must form outside for hours at a time before even entering the office. It is tiring, a waste of time, hugely embarrassing, and leaves them vulnerable to comments from passers by. Bob hopes that if they find a way to protest as a group, this requirement may be dropped. If the lot of the others is also changed for the better, so be it, but that does not matter to him. If this attitude is commonplace within the group's members, then the shared knowledge, the common goal, and the united action, even taken together, are insufficient to capture a morally rich sense of solidarity. The point of the hypothetical example is not of course that those receiving social assistance are selfish, but that even in the case of comembers of an oppressed group, we need to speak about the relationship between them and the attitudes they hold toward one another if we are to move to a morally rich conception of solidarity. Very little at all about that relationship is indicated by the simple facts that they share a common form of oppression and share some goals aimed at ending or lessening it.

Relationship between the Privileged and the Oppressed

At this point I want temporarily set aside the notion of solidarity among victims of oppression and bite the bullet by considering the most challenging context in situations of oppression, namely within the relationship between members of an oppressed group and relatively powerful, non-oppressed others, and see what we can learn here about a rich conception of moral solidarity. What kind of morally desirable relationship between the better-situated individuals and those who are systematically subordinated could reasonably be called one of solidarity? This discussion will point to the central role of empathetic understanding in my conception of moral solidarity.

A basic fact here is that the life-situation of the privileged is radically different from that of the oppressed and that holds in the case of civilized oppression, not only in cases of violent oppression. A privileged person can be thoughtful, well intentioned, and warm-hearted and yet know nothing about what it is like to live a life of denigration, exploitation, or exclusion. Consider for example the battles that took place before "stalking" was considered a significant wrong. Most stalking victims were and still are women. When early on in the fight, to have it taken seriously, they tried to explain what it was like to be constantly followed, to see the person standing outside their home all night, to find, repeatedly, abusive messages on their answering machine, and so on, many well-placed men responded with impatience. "Why," they asked, "are we supposed to bother about this when there are victims of real assault out there? It isn't as though these women are being harmed. Really, it's a lot of fuss about nothing." Such dismissive responses were heard on all sides. Many who had never been stalked and who could not see themselves ever at risk in this way trivialized the phenomena and were deeply resistant to correcting their misconception.

At this point the distinction between sheer information and empathetic understanding becomes central. So far as sheer knowledge is concerned, many affluent North Americans lack the most basic information of what is involved in, say, living in poverty, even in their own country— how much money on average the bottom 10 percent have, what the most minimal shelter costs to rent in various cities, what kind of food and other essential supplies can be bought with what remains, whether or not they can afford a phone, what they have by way of clothes and how long they keep them, and what having access only to public transport does to your mobility, security, and use of time, and so on. Having such information, though, does not mean that you are in solidarity with the destitute (who surely constitute a greatly oppressed group). It does not in itself ensure the relevant kind of "understanding." Such knowledge (which is largely lacking in those who are socially advantaged) is not enough.

In *Inessential Woman*, Elizabeth Spelman calls on the privileged to try to understand, to imagine, what the daily life of an oppressed person is like. "Imagination isn't enough, but it is necessary. Indeed, it is a crucial starting point,"[4] but she is aware that without the right relationship in place, the socially advantaged can use their imagination unilaterally to create an image or account that is wildly inaccurate.[5] "[T]he acquisition of such knowledge requires a kind of apprenticeship; and making oneself an apprentice to someone is at odds with having political, social, and economic power over them."[6] Two points are hovering here. First, the kind of "knowledge" (or "understanding") the advantaged should have should come from the oppressed. They are to learn from them. Second, they should try to imagine what it is like to live such a life, rather then, presumably, simply hear and note the basic observable information in a detached data-gathering mode. Sheer knowledge of that kind is not what Spelman's understanding is about.

Spelman is surely right that for these two goals to succeed, the stance of elitism, privilege, and the sense of being so sure about everything has to be released and this does not come easily to those whose word is routinely taken as reliable or even authoritative. Also, occasions for interaction may not naturally arise. A politician who grew up in a middle-class household, who has always lived in affluence, and who now holds the position of cabinet minister, not only has never lived in poverty but may never have interacted for more than a few seconds at a time with anyone who has. Given the lifestyle enjoyed, this pattern will probably continue indefinitely, unless the minister shows some initiative and also commits significant time to the role of careful listener. There is little that is obvious in a practical sense (as distinct from a moral sense) to prompt such commitments.

In the title of his paper, "Moral Deference," Laurence Thomas provides us with a memorable term for this kind of learning:

> It is a mode of moral learning which those who have been oppressed are owed in the name of eliminating the very state of their oppression. In the absence of such learning, oppression cannot but continue to be a part of the fabric of the moral life. Indeed, the absence of such learning, the studied refusal to engage in such learning, is one of the very ways in which oppression manifests itself. Worse, such studied refusal to learn adds insult to injury.[7]

What should the privileged learn about? A great deal more than the straightforwardly observable social facts of the oppression. Thomas explains that "It is not so much the brute facts of the social reality that need to be grasped, but the way in which that social reality impacts upon the lives of the group members—the emotional configuration of persons in the group."[8] How does one's life-situation affect one's emotional make-up? To use an example from Thomas, the vast majority of men do not think about the possibility of being attacked and raped when walking alone at night, although such an event is conceivable. On the other hand many women walking alone in the dark do think of and fear this possibility and "the difference here marks a difference in the emotional configuration between women and men, of equally good character."[9]

This does not mean that every woman's emotional configuration is the same. Individual events of a hostile or degrading kind and memories of them will leave their emotional mark, what Thomas calls "the subjective *imprimatur* of a category person's [oppressed person's] untoward experiences."[10] This said, the emotional configurations of members of an oppressed group are likely to have significant elements in common. To understand someone living such a subordinated life, then, is both to know the kinds of social facts they live with and to understand the emotional configuration that arises in response.

Thomas writes that "Moral deference...is the act of listening that is preliminary to bearing witness to another's moral pain."[11] Although he sometimes refers to moral deference as an act, it is clear from his paper as a whole that the attitude is crucial. Listening to the stories of the oppressed should not occur in a detached mode, nor with an attitude of curiosity or ridicule, nor with some self-interested goal in mind, but rather "letting another's pain re-constitute one so much so that one comes to have a new set of sensibilities—a new set of moral lenses if you will."[12] It is a kind of opening to another that is incompatible with being arrogant, scornful, or self-centered. As Sandra Bartky vividly remarks in her essay, "Sympathy and Solidarity," "what women, in particular feminists, demand from many men, I venture, is a knowing that transforms the self who knows, a knowing that brings into being new sympathies, new affects as well as new cognitions and new forms of intersubjectivity."[13] The hope is that not only will knowledge be acquired, but so too will empathetic understanding, and that in consequence a new kind of relationship will be developed.

Empathetic understanding, then, plays a central role in my conception of moral solidarity. Thinking back, then, on comembers of an oppressed group, empathetic understanding does indeed have a role to play there too. In our example, Bob is making use of his fellow victims solely to try to make his own situation better. They are fellow victims, but Bob sees no other bond between them. In our example we would not expect him to be a sympathetic listener to them when they have concerns (unless there was some gain to be had by pretending to do so). Shared experiences or not, we would not expect him to have any genuine empathy with them, given his exclusive self-focus. Yet such attempts at empathetic understanding are surely a form of basic respect that displays a basic concern for them and a wish for an improved situation for more than himself. In short, too much is lacking in Bob's relationship to his fellows to construe his relationship to them as one of moral solidarity.

The Non-Oppressed and the Oppressed: The Role of Moral Deference

As valuable as I believe Thomas's concept of moral deference to be, there is one significant danger I wish to explain, since otherwise we can easily overrestrict our notion of moral solidarity.

How should we conceive of the relationship between moral deference and moral solidarity? As mentioned earlier, given the current state of the literature, I am seeking a plausible reading of moral solidarity that captures something morally desirable, a reason for its desirability, and one or two morally interesting implications. I center moral solidarity around the relationship of empathetic understanding (something generally welcomed in feminist philosophy), but the more interesting points are perhaps to do with the implications.

It is tempting to think that privileged people can be in moral solidarity with members of an oppressed group only if they are morally deferential to them and that empathetic understanding (here proposed as the core of moral solidarity) requires such moral deference. But to make moral deference (to the stories told by the oppressed), a necessary condition of moral solidarity would bring with it a morally dubious implication I see no reason to be burdened with. It also involves too heavy a focus on "paternalism." I will explain both these concerns.

Making moral deference in the sense explained above, a necessary condition of moral solidarity restricts the conception in a disturbing way. Politicians giving time and careful attention to the stories of the long-time unemployed or men being increasingly willing to listen carefully to the stories women have to tell, and doing so in order to empathetically understand what it is like to be systematically disadvantaged, are paradigm examples of moral deference at work and the beginning of a relationship of solidarity between the two groups. Listening to people's stories, though, means that the storytellers are articulate, that they can in fact tell their stories. But "the oppressed" (in an inclusive sense covering all forms of oppression) and "those subject to civilized oppression" (in therefore a narrower sense) cover more than certain groups of articulate people who can speak carefully about their experiences. Many of the classic forms of even civilized oppression include inarticulate victims. It would be morally shortsighted to tie moral solidarity between the advantaged and the oppressed too tightly to the kind of moral deference that involves listening to careful explanations and personal accounts, since it would forestall any notion of solidarity in cases where the victims are unable to recount their experiences.

You do not have to be articulate in a rich sense to be oppressed. The seriously mentally challenged, those suffering from certain mental or physical illnesses, like advanced Alzheimer's, young children and more, are all vulnerable to systematic abuse and neglect and also subject to the more subtle forms of denigration and subordination that fall within the sphere of civilized oppression, yet they are unable to tell their stories in the usual way. Children, animals, and others are subjected to systematic cruelty, shameful neglect, scorn, dismissal, and contempt. Animals cannot give their accounts in a literal sense, and many infants and young children will either not acquire the ability to do so or, in some cases, simply not survive into young adulthood, to an age when they can speak more fully. Does it make sense to speak of being in moral solidarity with them? The very fact that they are so constrained in their ability to communicate is one fact that makes them very different from cases where the paradigmatic advocate, protestor, or activist—those who would move into a relationship of solidarity with them—would act. Does difference, even major difference, eliminate the possibility of a relationship that could legitimately be called solidarity? I will argue below that it does not and I reject as a necessary condition anything that restricts solidarity to a relationship between two fully articulate parties.

Too Heavy a Focus on "Paternalism"

When we urge an attitude of moral deference in the case of articulate victims of oppression, it is often because we are concerned about an all too frequent and objectionable alternative—that of high-handed paternalism. We may be tempted to make this kind of deference a necessary condition of moral solidarity because of this concern. It is not unusual for those who have not been at the receiving end of systematic exclusion and subordination to inform the victims of what "really happened" at gatherings they did not attend, what the key players "really meant" when they said this or that, what the most reasonable response would have been, and even how the victims should have felt in situations they themselves have never been in. There is nothing of Spelman's apprentice relationship here.

Someone in a privileged position may claim to be in solidarity with a group experiencing injustice, but if the person's thinking is developed without interaction of the right kind with the victims, the danger of misperception, oversights, and the imposition of false descriptions on the relevant phenomena are all too familiar. Even if genuinely concerned about injustice and benevolently motivated, confused perceptions and a lack of understanding are predictable, given the systematic differences in life experience. Goodwill is far from enough. It is classic paternalism and however unintentionally, it embodies deep disrespect for the oppressed. Used in this way, paternalism is a pejorative term and refers to something inherently morally untoward.

In some cases those closest to the victims are the most likely to move into this pattern, precisely because they wish the victim well. If some distressing experience can be traced to some mistake on the part of the person herself, perhaps an error of judgment or some overreaction, then this means there is a way to avoid such distress in the future—by making more careful judgments or by bring keeping a better sense of proportion in similar situations when such situations arise in future. Objectionable, paternalistic victim-blaming does not require a hostile agent.[14]

However, unless we insist that only fully articulate people can be involved in relationships of moral solidarity, the fear of this pernicious form of paternalism should not completely dominate a discussion of solidarity. It is important where the oppressed are indeed able to explain to others their life-experiences and how they affect their prospects, their thoughts, feelings, hopes, and dreams, but this is not always possible. If paternalism is standardly used as a pejorative term—something that is, by definition, morally wrong—then we need a different and neutral term for a relationship where the actions and *some* aspects of the attitude of paternalism may be morally appropriate. For this I will refer to a relationship of "protective aid" and there are situations where the protective mode is morally sound.

Protective Aid and the Kind of Learning about the Other It Involves

In many cases, elderly people whose mental functioning has seriously deteriorated are routinely left for most of the day in a fog of isolation and despair or drugged into semi-consciousness or tied down to a bed or wheelchair for the convenience of those responsible for their well-being.

This neglect and indeed cruelty is why people in some societies are terrified of becoming old and mentally infirm. Animals too are systematically mistreated, killed, even tortured all around the world in the name of education, professional training, product safety, food production, sport, entertainment, pharmaceutical testing, and more. In these and other instances the victims' inherent vulnerability makes them easy targets, but they are not able to explain the nature of their abuse and how it affects them, to protest their wrongs, and to call for radical change. Concerned others must take the initiative and we should beware of letting the specter of paternalism loom too large. A relationship of protective aid is morally sound in such cases.

The relationship has its special challenges, given that the ideal of a first person, full account of the misery is not accessible. Still, such victims do signal their pain, terror, deep frustration, and despair, but without being able to tell their stories in the usual sense. So the would-be advocates can certainly fail to qualify as sound advocates, they can fail to do what is reasonably required in lieu of listening to the accounts of these victims. There can be far too little by way of observation and interaction and initiative on the part of those who would be their advocates. "Speaking" (whether vocally, by sign language, or by some form of writing, etc.) is not the only way to signal great distress, but often one must learn about trends within such signals to begin to come to grips with their distress. Terrified or despairing animals tend to assume certain body positions over and above any vocalizations they make. Anyone who has entered into a close relationship with companion animals becomes aware of these and other, more subtle signals of how things are for them. Furthermore, indications of the causes of the distress or fear or lack of confidence, and so on, can be conveyed without standard articulation. We can observe that our rescued and formerly abused dog is afraid of any man with a moustache. Or a dog who has visited the veterinary clinic without significant distress for some years suddenly trembles and tries to hide when walking in and seeing the new vet for the second time. Our caring for them involves being alert to these "communications" and such clues need not be intentionally conveyed to be successfully apprehended. Nonetheless, if a description in the usual sense is to be given, it will come from concerned others, except for special cases where the inability to explain is temporary or reversible (e.g., children who grow up to adulthood may be able to recount their childhood nightmares, and it is at least conceivable that one day something like advanced Alzheimer's will be reversible). In the cases that are central to my point here, there is no later time when the victims will acquire such an ability. Any description or explanation will inevitably embody the judgment of non-victim others.

In the best of circumstances there will be genuine concern, engagement, and discussion with other concerned people (especially those who have been actively involved in advocacy or aid of one kind or another for some time), a willingness to set aside preconceived assumptions and to do one's homework on background information (although caution is needed as to who "the experts" really are), and other attempts to reach careful and thoughtful accounts of what is wrong and what needs to be changed. The challenge becomes greater the less that outright violence, confinement, or deprivation of the basics of life (food, water, shelter) are involved, that is, the closer the situations parallel those of civilized oppression. Even so, we can often know that things are terribly wrong for someone (even for a nonhuman someone) without being in a position to know and describe the full scope of the misery and the nuances of the pain, fear, and desolation. We can also have every reason to believe that the one suffering lacks the power to change the situation.

So there is a kind of caring attentiveness owed to such victims, but it is significantly different from deferring to their personal accounts of their experiences (Thomas's rich sense of moral deference), and, at least in the central cases—those I am focusing on here—it inevitably involves a much bigger contribution from concerned others. In fact the term "deference" hardly fits the situation. Great attention and concern is owed the victims and their suffering, but they make no pronouncements others should defer to and there are no consultations where the approval of the victims must be given, not because we would not wish to do so, but because by the nature of the case it cannot be done. There is nothing in fact that places the victims in a classically construed "authoritative" role as distinct from a morally central role. If actions are to be taken to change the situation of these victims, then except for articulate adults who were once child victims, it will be on the basis of the best judgments made by non-victims who have placed themselves in a protective relationship with the victims. Such relationships are morally sound even though there is always some risk of misunderstanding or misperceiving.

Can fully articulate advocates and those working for reform be in moral solidarity with oppressed individuals who are dramatically "different" from themselves? One of the most challenging cases here is the relationship between humans with the usual range of mental abilities and animals. Clearly we cannot be in moral solidarity with animals if we insist on the rich sense of moral deference as a necessary condition of such a relationship, if we insist that a relationship of protective aid is incompatible with moral solidarity. But I see no reason to agree to this.

Animals are systematically abused to the point of torture in every continent in a number of longstanding practices. Their terror and suffering and despair are transparent to all but those willfully in denial, many of whom have deeply vested interests in not acknowledging the obvious. Their denial allows them to continue with their long-time teaching practices, with their customary forms of entertainment, with their ability to maximize profits as a pharmaceutical business or as a farmer, and with their ability to sleep at night. We can learn not only of the transparent misery, but of more subtle kinds of suffering if we place ourselves in the role of someone who open-mindedly wishes to learn. In spite of centuries of interaction with elephants, it is only recently that the depth of their emotional lives has begun to be understood, for example, their ability to feel deep and life-long grief for a slaughtered member of their family.

Such learning has arisen because a few people have set aside preconceived stereotypes, braved the scorn of their peers, and had the courage to approach the animals in a spirit of humility, to see if there are things to learn. Furthermore, they could not have learned about the grief of elephants if they had not had an attitude of empathy, a willingness to conceive of the animals' having deep feelings, and a willingness to imaginatively enter into those feelings as much as possible. Learning of this kind profoundly moves the learner, especially when suffering is involved, and in this sense, it has the hallmark of the kind of learning Thomas refers to (above) when speaking of his paradigm cases of moral deference, that of "letting another's pain re-constitute one so much so that one comes to have a new set of sensibilities—a new set of moral lenses if you will." It is a far cry from detached information gathering. Animals are fellow sufferers in this world and insofar as their pain is systematic and attributable to misguided, callous, or outright cruel people, they constitute a greatly oppressed group consisting of some of the most vulnerable individuals in the world. It is speciesist simply to declare that we cannot be in a relationship of moral solidarity with them because they are not human or because they cannot give first-hand, fully articulate accounts of their lives. Centering moral solidarity around empathetic understanding does not prohibit such relationships from holding between humans and animals. We can have a bond with them as fellow sufferers, even though they cannot fully articulate their experiences and cannot take up the fight for their own rescue. It is the empathetic understanding of their pain and fear that prompts us to join victims in their struggle against oppression or to take protective action on their behalf, if that is all that can be done. In both cases the actions follow morally from the relationship of empathetic understanding and solidarity with the suffering victims. Our ability to be in moral solidarity with animals and others who lack the capacity to "tell their stories" is one of the significant implications of the position.

Civilized oppression involves harms and wrongs that lack the eye-catching violence found in dramatic cases of oppression, and for this reason Thomas's moral deference is vital (where indeed it can be entered into). Physical attack is so much more straightforward to take seriously than persistent verbal denigration or persistent exclusion. There is a lot to learn in both kinds of cases, but in the latter we often have to learn that there is anything at all worth learning.

Not all civilized oppression involves articulate victims, and relationships of moral solidarity between non-oppressed observers and those victims may sometimes involve stages of "protective aid" and advocacy that are not based on standard moral deference (because they cannot be). The core of moral solidarity as I have argued for is empathetic understanding, but this relationship is compatible with that of protective aid in certain circumstances.

Civilized Oppression and Contributing Agents

I will argue for a second, yet more controversial, claim. Civilized oppression is the most pervasive form of oppression in Western societies and by its nature, it is hard to perceive. It can take subtle forms that are relentlessly persistent and it wrecks lives. It is inherently difficult for the socially advantaged to be aware at all of the phenomena involved, let alone their impact on the victims. Indeed, victims themselves often do not readily take in what is happening. Understanding what is involved means understanding the kinds of mechanisms used, the power relations at work, the systems controlling perceptions and information, the kinds of harms and wrongs inflicted on the victims, and the correlation between systematic mistreatment and cumulative harm and degradation, and all without the signs of physical violence that so starkly demand our moral attention in the case of less subtle forms of oppression.

There might not even be any overt name-calling, no one may be yelling, and no one may be writing slogans on the wall. Much of what is done that sustains the oppression is socialized into the contributing agents and is a matter of habitual behavior. When a conversation leaves an opening for a joke about bossy and bad tempered mothers-in-law, Dave cannot resist supplying such a joke. When a similar opportunity arises for a joke about fathers-in-law, it passes him by completely unnoticed, since there is no cultural practice of such jokes. He is totally unaware of this difference in his behavior. Or consider a small business where several women employees have been hired recently. At staff meetings, the business owner, who has chaired these meetings for over 40 years, habitually takes the first few questions or comments from the male employees, even though the women signal more quickly that they have things to say. He does not know he does this. Or again, when it is Ms. Taylor's turn for her appointment with the dentist, he addresses her as "Christine," unaware that whenever the client is male, the form of address changes to "Mr. Jones" or "Mr. Morelli."

There is a type of civilized oppression that is heavily socialized and unthinkingly sustained. The agents do not plan to harm anyone; they have no explicit intention to disadvantage those they actually victimize. Seemingly small actions and omissions occur repeatedly and relentlessly to members of the vulnerable groups and any one of the incidents would be trivial were it not for the fact that it is part of an entrenched pattern, which over time systematically harms, marginalizes, denigrates, and demoralizes its victims. Contributing agents in these cases can be warm hearted, goodwilled, and in more straightforward ways—where nothing subtle is involved—benevolent. They may give very generously to the victims of a natural disaster, they will rush to help someone who has slipped on the ice, and they are never tempted to use violence against anyone (except perhaps in a life-threatening defense situation). They would be shocked to hear themselves described as oppressors, yet they are. Their privileged position shields them from a face-to-face encounter with the effects of their oppression, since many victims are wary of being completely open and forthright with such powerfully placed people (powerful relative to themselves).

In such cases it is not simply a matter of the privileged not understanding how what they are doing can have such devastating effects on people's lives and feelings. It goes one step further back. In a literal sense, they are unaware of their actions. Becoming aware involves perceptual skills they do not yet have and which they so far have no motivation to acquire. The employer is totally unaware of giving unfair preference to his male employees at the meetings. His actions are deeply ingrained as a 40-year-old habit.

How frequent is this kind of unawareness? Setting aside oppression for a moment, it is a daily phenomenon that surfaces time and again. A student writes a seven-page paper and irritatingly uses the term "scenario" eight times. She is taken completely by surprise when this word addiction is mentioned. A conference speaker fielding questions from the audience always plays with the ring on his finger when the question is unsettling—either very difficult or rather abrasive—something he never does with questions that he is at ease with. He has no knowledge that he is signaling when he is feeling "hedged in" by a questioner. Just about everyone has habits she is unaware of until she makes an effort to sharpen the perceptual skill involved in detecting them, or unless someone else draws attention to them. In the cases of interest here, it involves more than, say, the irritating overuse of a favored word. The unperceived habits sustain oppression. The point, though, is that this phenomenon of unawareness is not intrinsically different in the two kinds of cases, the innocuous and the oppressive.

Victims themselves can find it difficult to pinpoint the relevant actions in the early stages of thinking about civilized oppression. Susan may come to dislike going to Frank's parties long before realizing that his tendency to tell jokes that denigrate women has a lot to do with it, or she may be unsure why she leaves the dentist's office with the impression that the dentist has more respect for men than for women.

It is vital that the oppressors' habits change, but can we not empathize with the one who does not see what he habitually does, at least not until the issue is addressed and attention is drawn to the habit? Not everyone's habits and socialized behavior are oppressive, but rare indeed is the person who is fully aware of all his actions, subtle habits and all (if such a person is to be found).

So I make the controversial claim that empathetic understanding can sometimes be morally appropriate not only between agents of oppression and the oppressed, but between the oppressed and at least some who are contributing agents of oppression, not because we should tolerate the oppression involved, but because lying behind it is a failing just about anyone who is ruthlessly honest can lay claim to, namely, being unaware of all our actions. It can show in nonmoral contexts and it can show in socialized and oppressive behavior.

In fact, it can show in the behavior of an oppressed victim of one group toward a member of another group. Being a victim of oppression does not bring with it an all-seeing awareness of everything one does—everything from how one votes to where one sits to glances given and nods withheld. Widespread and ongoing patterns within the most trivial-looking actions can and sometimes do constitute systematic discrimination, the impact and significance of which usually escapes the notice of the contributing agents and non-oppressed bystanders. Oppressed victims are not immune to this problem. None of us is fully and permanently alert to our own behavior, although we can become more self-aware with effort and over time. Empathetic understanding is, I suggest, appropriate in some cases involving agents who contribute, all unknown to themselves, to civilized oppression, especially where those involved are trying to become more self-aware.

How does this connect with relationships of moral solidarity? Forming such a relationship with the victims of oppression can involve various kinds of "learning," empathetic understanding of their experiences, and actions toward lessening or ending their oppression. We are in solidarity with them "against their oppression." This does not mean "against their oppressors" if there are at least some (and I emphasize "some") agents of oppression who, for reasons given above, may themselves deserve empathetic understanding. That is, there are some kinds of cases where there is a significant difference between the two ways of speaking. The question this raises is whether we can appropriately be in moral solidarity not only with victims of oppression, but with an agent of oppression (while being deeply committed to ending the oppressive situation or practice). I believe so.

I have argued that some agents of civilized oppression are understandably unaware of their ongoing contribution to it and that since the underlying faults shared by everyone, we can appropriately form relationships of moral solidarity with them even while insisting that they begin the work to end their contributions. In the cases referred to, the major failing is that of acting on deeply ingrained socialized habits the agent is unaware of. Michele Moody-Adams has a far less sympathetic view of the role of socialized practices in contributing to oppression. She refers to the view that "cultural influences can excuse wrongdoing in virtue of their tendency to produce nonculpable ignorance,"[15] and emphatically denies this. It is, says Moody-Adams, "affected ignorance," which is "essentially a matter of choosing not to be informed of what we can and should know."[16] With respect to the examples Moody-Adams works with—Greek slavery, torture, and Nazi concentration camps, I agree that the fact that the practices are culturally embedded cannot excuse people from leaving either their involvement or the practice itself unexamined.

The nature of these examples, though, matters a great deal here. They are horrifically violent and, at least in principle, highly visible. No one can sincerely claim not to know that he is placing two Jewish inmates back to back to see if he can kill both with one bullet through their heads (which happened at Auschwitz); no one can claim not to be aware of the screams as he electrocutes a political prisoner. Socially endorsed or not, claiming to be unaware of anything so egregiously wrong is affected ignorance. Anything so shocking, especially where one is directly involved, cries out for a revolt from the core of one's being (hopefully with many hours of deep and critical scrutiny thereafter).

Moody-Adams' examples (Greek slavery, torture, and Nazi concentration camps) are about as far away from the instances of civilized oppression I write about as one could imagine. Violence always calls for rigorous justification. Furthermore, civilized oppression itself covers quite a range of phenomena and acts, from flat refusals to go upstairs to take the medicine to the sick child to doodling in a notebook every time one of the women panelists speaks (but not when a man does). Our "culture" affects our pre-reflective actions and attitudes, but there are serious moral dangers in generalizing across all forms of actions and beliefs relevant to oppression. Civilized oppression is highly effective in wrecking the lives of its victims, but the absence of violence can make it much harder to "see" its oppressive nature.

Even within civilized oppression there are significant moral differences between the phenomena at one end of the range and those at the other. The more blatant the action and the more obviously connected with civilized forms of ageism, sexism, racism, or some other type, the more plausible is Moody-Adams' point. Overt refusals to go to the store and buy diapers, or change a diaper, or spend time with a fretful, sick child in the evening, or feed the young child or clean up the predictable mess on the table afterward, clearly signal the belief that it is not for the "man of the house" to take on the tasks of raising a toddler. Yet he can and, I agree with Moody-Adams, should know what the implications of this steadfast refusal are for the woman caregiver. This is especially so given how much this and related issues have been seriously discussed in recent decades. On the other hand, at the other, extreme end of civilized oppression even being aware of one's actions at all, given their subtlety, is unlikely until a lot of work is done on developing perceptual skills of self-awareness. In the ordinary run of things, we do not notice when we raise an eyebrow or glance to the person beside me or nod encouragingly to the speaker (or equally, refrain from doing so), and in the ordinary run of things this is fine. Such actions either have no moral bearing or they occur in morally appropriate ways. But if there are persistent patterns of discrimination and selectivity, then there is no doubt that these completely "innocent trivialities" can systematically discourage members of one group while encouraging those of another, alert some to some social or professional hazard while letting others wade into deep waters, nodding some in the direction of some vital information while leaving others to manage without, and so on. That is to say, very subtle actions that the agent does not know he does can and do form systematic patterns of civilized oppression. It is understandable if the agents are not aware of their very actions, let alone their consequences. At *this* point, what we are dealing with is not affected ignorance, which Moody-Adams clarifies as "choosing not to be informed of what we can and should know." The pressing issue it not to do with information and knowledge (an issue that may arise at a later point.) Right now at this end of the civilized oppression spectrum, it is the lack of perceptual acuity about one' own "small" actions, the absence of the crucial kind of perceptual ability, that makes it understandable that they do not see their role in the oppression.

Benson's Objection

There will be predictable objections to this way of seeing this group of agents who contribute to the less visible (but serious) instances of civilized oppression. I have in mind the extreme end of the civilized oppression spectrum where a literal lack of awareness of one's apparently insignificant actions is functioning. Paul Benson raises concerns about how we think of agents who have been heavily socialized into oppressive habits, and in particular points to what he sees as an implication about the "moral work" lessening oppression involves.[17] He refers to

> persons who conform and contribute to oppressive practices in part because their capacities to recognize ethically significant features of their circumstances are deficient. Their competence to perceive the wrongs committed in those practices and to imagine ethically

preferable social alternatives has been stunted by the early social training that prepared them to accept, and perhaps defend, injustice (under more attractive descriptions).[18]

The first important thing to point out is that Benson's description covers a much wider range of the civilized oppression spectrum than does my point above. I am particularly interested in the role that highly developed perceptual skills play in sometimes being an oppressive agent, skills that are extremely unlikely to develop without explicit and long-term effort and commitment. If I consistently, say, look at the men in the meeting to seek their input first without "seeing" that I routinely overlook at this initial stage the women who are signaling their wish to speak, then I am unaware of how I glance around the room at the beginnings of these meetings. This is a problem, but I suggest that it is rather different with respect to the role of fairly sophisticated perceptual awareness skills than, say, a man sitting in a chair all evening, watching TV, and watching his wife run upstairs repeatedly to look after their sick child. I have in mind here the common social practice of holding the mother responsible for looking after an ill child, a practice so commonly accepted that advertisements of children's medicines are all aimed at women viewers (e.g., the Dr. Mom advertisements). Whether or not he notices that this is happening, there is still quite a radical difference in the kinds of perceptions involved and many such situations are not included in the range I have in mind with my point above.

Still, I wish to take up one of the implications that Benson mentions, since perhaps it could apply to the cases I have in mind. He points out that heavily socialized oppressors "seem to deserve to be released from responsibility for actions motivated partly by their patchy moral blindness."[19] If so, then

Since they can claim to be sufficiently capable moral agents in most of the rest of their lives, their exemption from blame in oppressive contexts frees them to limit their attention and concern to matters on which their competence has been socially certified. As a result, the difficult ethical labor of uncovering, analyzing, articulating, and struggling to resist the wrongs these oppressors perpetuate passes to others...In practice, then, the demands for moral work that arise from blameless oppressors' activities are likely to fall most heavily on a small group of the oppressed.[20]

However, it is unclear that the oppressive agents are simply "exempt from blame," either in the wide range of socialized, oppressive practices that Benson seems to have in mind, or indeed in the cases where the role of developed perceptual self-awareness is critical and far higher (the kinds of cases I refer to). One can understand the lack of such awareness and we can in all honesty find examples of the same problem in ourselves, even if perhaps the gaps in our self-awareness do not function oppressively. Having analogous experiences allows us to empathize with those in whom the lack does function oppressively. None of this, though, means that we are obliged to leave the moral story there and conclude that the agents, morally speaking, are "home free" and that nothing more is to be said.

There is no preset number of "stages" of reflection that a moral situation calls for. Yes, in a way, it is one stage of reflection to note that in the cases of extreme range of civilized oppression, those that are my primary concern here, we can legitimately and empathetically understand that the contributing agents do not perceive what their various actions are, let alone what their impact is when they are ongoing and systematic. But as soon as those actions are perceived by someone, whether some of the victims, some non-oppressed observers, or an atypical agent of civilized oppression, we are obliged to move to the second stage of reflection where it becomes clear that precisely because so much is understandably missed in these situations (and often by more than the agents themselves), we must take far more seriously a moral obligation to develop certain perceptual skills. And skills are much involved. Neither goodwill nor an overall good moral disposition is enough in these cases.

These agents are not morally innocent in any robust sense. Since our actions, any and all of them, can affect others, it is not difficult to speak of a prima facie obligation to be far more fully aware of what we do, say, and behaviorally indicate than is possible without committed and long-term effort. Except for readily seen actions, this may not even have been thought about by these agents. With respect to the less visible (but nonetheless highly effective) actions, they move through daily life blissfully unaware of what they systematically do, of the unspoken messages they convey, and of the harms their actions bring about. It should be remembered that civilized oppression of this type is extremely commonplace and cumulatively very effective, whether intended to be or not. It is by no means a rare or even unusual matter. Being oblivious to the moral call to be a lot more self-aware about our own actions is a significant moral oversight and as such a failing, but if we can justifiably empathize only with those free of such failings, then empathy will be thin on the ground indeed.

And we should not confuse the moral issues with straightforwardly empirical matters. When I claim that we have a moral obligation to work on being more aware of our own actions, I am not of course saying that everyone will be willing to do so or that everyone will leap at the chance to work on this. As things are, civilized oppression is still much overlooked and its importance much underrated when seen at all. This is predictably accompanied by deep resistance to taking it seriously, to reflecting on it, and to making major changes. Benson claims that the "ethical labor of uncovering, analyzing, articulating, and struggling to resist the wrongs these oppressors perpetuate" passes to "a small group of the oppressed" (see note 19). The work on civilized oppression in Western societies is at a relatively early stage and it is therefore, indeed, articulate victims who are the prime movers in morally addressing it. Thomas's insistence that "moral deference" be accorded them and Spelman's call for the privileged, non-oppressed to become "apprentices" in learning about forms of oppression are both indicators of the moral work to be done, which at this stage is crucially reliant on the initiatives of articulate victims. It may not be "fair" in any ideal-world sense, but it is how major reforms gain momentum. None of this excuses either agents or non-oppressed non-victims from moving their reflections and in fact their "learning" to the next stage: to the realization that although some of our oversights are completely understandable, they nonetheless constitute moral failings and that we therefore face obligations to tackle them. Moral analysis standardly involves such stages and there is nothing incompatible about the "first" and "second" stage referred to above. We can be accountable not only for our lack of knowledge, but more pertinently here, for our lack of perceptual ability.

The Underlying Value of the Relationship

Moral solidarity here is not the same as "working against systematic injustice" or "supporting the victims in their struggle against their oppression." I can perform such actions for a number of reasons, including self-interest. Moral solidarity construed as a relationship (as it is here) involves both parties; it cannot be focused solely on "the self" in the relationship. Suppose that I am engaging in such actions because of concern for the victims and because I believe that what they are going through is immoral. Is this enough to justify claiming to be in moral solidarity with them? I think that even here the bond can be too weak. You have told me that they are suffering persistent injustice and I know from years of experience that your judgment and sense of fairness are excellent, and so I believe you and I am therefore concerned about the victims. I offer to help and I spend many hours responding willingly to the requests made of me, but throughout the years of volunteer work, I am never asked to do anything that depends on having a deep understanding of their situation and the nature of the unfairness they experience. I think of and organize a series of fund-raising events, none of them placing me in the role of a key-speaker. I provide transport for anyone and everyone connected to the group and its struggle, to and from the airport, across town, to stores to pick up posters, coffee urns, and chairs. I give a great deal of time, money, and energy to the cause. Certainly I am providing support, but unless there is a difference between support and being in a relationship of moral solidarity, the latter term is redundant. In particular, support can be sincere, active, costly, and well motivated and still not involve empathetic understanding—and on the conception offered here, moral solidarity involves that relationship. If we think of "political solidarity" with the oppressed as sustained and supportive action aimed at ending oppression, then it is not as morally rich an account as it might first appear if it is not anchored in something like what I have called moral solidarity.

As discussed in the literature on oppression, the usual "direction" of the relationship of empathetic understanding (and so moral solidarity) holds between the privileged and the oppressed victims. Why it is morally desirable for the privileged to be in a relationship of empathetic understanding with oppressed victims? For one thing, such understanding will probably open up more by way of action that the socially advantaged could contribute. If enough of the advantaged engage in the relationship, it may bring about an earlier end to the oppression. But even consequences such as these, worthy as they are, are not where I locate the true value of moral solidarity. I see building a relationship of empathetic understanding as an expression of caring and respect for the victims in their own right, and it is because of that respectful caring that we are motivated to work to improve their lot. I emphasize empathetic understanding as prima facie desirable in its own right over simply learning from the victims in the name of ending the oppression, because the two can involve a rather subtle difference in attitude. In both cases there is attentiveness, genuine interest, and quite possibly selfless concern for what is right, but it is one thing to be seen as a source of education, even on such a vital issue as oppression, and another to be seen as someone who matters in her own right.

But the relationship of empathetic understanding can hold in the other direction too. In certain circumstances non-divisive relationships can be built between victims of civilized oppression and at least some of the contributing agents. Indeed, we should beware of setting the moral bar too high. A community is partly a place where we support each other in our imperfection and failings, which is the common lot of humans. Without supporting the oppressive and unnoticed habits, I can build a relationship of moral solidarity with someone of goodwill who, all unknown, has habits that are contributing to injustice, especially where perceptual inability plays a key role. We recognize the fellowship of the fellow-oppressed, but even when so oppressed, we are also all of us fellow strugglers with our own failings and oversights and (hopefully) moral progress to make. That is something victims share with the kind of contributing agent being referred to, the one who is functioning at the extreme end of the spectrum of civilized oppression. Empathetic support of the right kind can be morally appropriate and may even be a factor in the agent's beginning to perceive his involvement in the oppression. The moral agency of the victims extends beyond that of resistance in the classic sense of protest and rebellion.

Limits on Moral Solidarity?

A relationship that involves empathetic understanding does not just happen. It requires active involvement with the other, undertaken with a willingness to learn and to try to feel another's pains and joys. Empathetic understanding will not always be mutual and in some cases cannot be (e.g., in some relationships with animals), but it may develop even if only one of the two parties has the ability and commitment needed to develop it. Such an engaged understanding will also sometimes bring with it the call to action, both big and small. Perhaps I need to speak with someone whom I believe has been misunderstood and who is now too embarrassed to speak herself and ask permission to speak on her behalf. Perhaps more systematic and political action is involved (and obviously one can only take on so many campaigns without collapse). So for these kinds of reasons, no matter how willing, we cannot in practice have empathetic understanding (in its developed sense) for everyone in the world, nor even for everyone we actually come in contact with.

Is this morally problematic? In "Sympathy and Solidarity," Sandra Bartky is particularly interested in the suffering of others and its relevance to political action, but the problems she raises have noticeable parallels to the issue here. She asks, "What is it, exactly, to become more 'sensitive' to the Other, in addition, that is, to my learning more about her circumstances?"[21] and then writes:

> since the kind of politics I am considering—feminist politics—bears an important relationship to human suffering in some, if not in all ways, does my emotional response to the suffering of others first select those others with whom I wish to be in solidarity? If I am right about the relationship between politics and suffering, and if, as is likely,

everyone suffers, on what basis can I offer myself to some sufferings and deny myself to others? And given the pervasiveness of suffering and the multitude of forms such suffering may take, how can I keep myself from getting so spent emotionally that I burn out and so turn out to be useless as a political agent?[22]

We cannot be blamed for what cannot be done and in practice there is a limit on the numbers of those with whom we can develop a relationship of empathetic understanding, but it is a morally pertinent matter how the "selection" should be made. In particular, the fact that the number is restricted does not mean that it should be kept to just "special relationships" (like family relationships or close friendships), nor that it is morally acceptable to do so. Other things being equal, it is a part of what family and friendship should involve, a key component of the kind of trust such relationships should nurture, and the kind of emotional security they should naturally provide, but there is something morally shallow if not callous about those who either cannot or will not empathetically understand anyone not in a close personal relationship with them. It is sweepingly dismissive of anyone not within their personal sphere of interest and it is also profoundly self-centered and morally arrogant. No one else is worth knowing in this special sense and there is no morally pressing reason for including others (e.g., one has nothing to learn from them).

Perhaps the most difficult question to answer satisfactorily is whether empathetic respect is inevitably limited not only by sheer numbers, but also by limits to empathy itself. Are there instances where it would be unreasonable to expect reflective and well-intentioned people to hold such an attitude once they begin to know the individual more fully? Could there be revealed such morally appalling things that natural human empathy evaporates? Could a stunningly low appraisal respect be justified and block the possibility of empathy? Could there be such revulsion that attempts to be empathetic collapse into failure? In practice, it happens, but the pertinent question is whether it should. In principle at least, should there be no limits to empathy? Some people who are morally conscientious, honest, and caring have apparently been able to hold something like this attitude in the most extraordinary circumstances.

The film, *Dead Man Walking*, portrays a nun who is a death row counselor and who develops empathy not only for the victim's family, but also for the murderer. It is based on fact and I gather it is quite accurate. Sister Helen Prejean has now counseled at least four convicted murderers whom she has accompanied to the death chamber. Perhaps, though, the theological underpinnings of her convictions are indispensable to her being able to show what seems to be genuine empathy for the murderers (while in no way condoning the murders). Perhaps, but I think it would be presumptuous to try to answer this.

Within the confines of this chapter I will go out on a limb and say that I think it is reasonable and not a moral fault if there is some point at which a person's attempt to form an empathetic relationship collapses because of something deeply disturbing and central about the other person, but I will also make a very modest point in the other direction, namely, that we should not be too hasty in assuming that empathetic understanding is impossible in the case of wrongdoers. Moral wrong comes in degrees, but when all is said and done, who is not a wrongdoer? If empathetic understanding is to be given only to the morally flawless, then it cannot be given. We are wiser, I think, to have the default position of being willing to develop empathetic understanding when suitable opportunities arise. New bonds are formed and existing bonds are deepened. Relationships may be mutual in the contributions the various parties make, or they may involve radical differences. Unlike economic exchanges, many of the "contributions" are spontaneously made with no thought to the joy or sadness or delight they may cause, others are the result of much thought or perhaps much courage. When a previously abused companion animal has in a dozen different ways revealed his terror and nightmares and a lot about the sources of them, when you begin to realize some of what he has been through in the systematic mistreatment and cruelty suffered as part of one of the standard and oppressive practices inflicted on such animals, when he eventually tries to trust once more, fearful still of being badly hurt and rejected, it becomes clear that our relationships of trying to achieve empathetic understanding come in many shapes. They can be mutual or asymmetrical relationships of learning or healing, of pain shared or joy rediscovered, but all of this and more is compatible with their being relationships of moral solidarity with individuals who have suffered systematic oppression. They constitute just one of the morally rich kinds of relationships that can help build community, both small and large, in ways that erode ignorance, indifference, preconceptions, and systematic wrong, and that open up new insights and fresh beginnings—and more individuals than are usually spoken of can be a party to such a relationship.

CHAPTER 4

Moral Community, Solidarity, and Civilized Oppression

Motivating the Conception of Moral Community

Appropriate relationships of moral solidarity enrich the notion of a moral community. The building of a moral community throughout our fragile world is a poignant vision, but the image that speaks to many of us is of a less chilly and more inclusive community than the traditional conception would have it. Here I am offering my conception of a moral community by giving free rein to some speculative thoughts and a few beginnings of my reasons for them. (It is the prelude to a much larger project.)

My conception of a moral community is motivated by two moral concerns: the care and protection of those who are vulnerable to suffering, especially, but not only, nonnatural suffering that arises as a result of human wrongdoing, and second, the empowerment, development, and support of thoughtful and intellectually honest moral agency. These two are deeply connected in that the moral obligations involved in taking seriously the first concern calls for a mature level of insightful moral agency, and that is not something a person is born with, nor is it something that inevitably arises at a certain age. To belong to the moral community I envisage, one need not be "a rational human being," a "person" in the philosophically traditional sense, nor even a human being at all. In her article, "At the Margins of Moral Personhood,"

Eva Feder Kittay writes that "rationality and the capacity to determine one's own good are, at the very least, useful to being a part of a moral community. But I am not sure if either is necessary, and I am still less certain why lacking them disqualifies one from moral parity."[1] With this I entirely agree (although there are other points in her article where we part company, e.g., on the moral status of animals) and although I cannot do justice to her paper here, she speaks movingly of her much loved daughter, born with a serious intellectual disability, showing the richness and significance of the relationship between herself and her daughter. For myself, I come to much the same issues from my close relationships with nonhuman individuals, found, rescued, defended, adopted, and mourned, but I cannot include these issues in my current work. I can only emphasize the diversity of those with whom we can enter into relationships of empathetic understanding and the actions that naturally follow.

Empathetic understanding is an appropriate initial response to vulnerability and suffering, followed by action that protects or aids in one way or another. One does not need to be a classical utilitarian to believe that suffering is bad and complete powerlessness in the face of great suffering deeply distressing. The moral community is not only where moral thinking and questioning are anchored, it is where the actual practice of the moral life finds expression. Those we should bear in mind when making decisions, those who have a call upon our consideration, empathetic understanding, and intervention, may not themselves be able to respond in kind. The vulnerable are often subject to suffering because of our actions without having the capacities of moral agents to any reasonable degree. If anything, this tends to render them even more vulnerable than many of the agent-members of the community; certainly they cannot literally remonstrate, protest, call upon others for help and support, and so on. Their acute vulnerability, especially to the agent-members, is sufficient reason not only for including them within the moral community, but seeing them at the very heart of why we need to think in terms of "community." They are vulnerable to our attitudes, our beliefs, our actions, and the implications of our moral character. On my conception of the moral community, more than those with a reasonable degree of moral agency are members. Included too are non-agent humans and many nonhuman animals. They belong not peripherally as some kind of courteous gesture, but at the center of the community and as of right, given their capacity to suffer, notably here at the hands of human agents. Empathetic understanding is a morally appropriate response, and although each agent has unavoidable limitations on the scope of that empathy, agents collectively can and should extend such empathetic understanding to the vulnerable of many and varied groups, including vulnerable others never seen by most of the agents with that empathetic attitude. Those subject to suffering at the hands of human agents have the right to our deepest consideration, since morally speaking we are answerable to our victims, and even if they cannot literally understand our supposed justifications and explanations, we are also answerable to the moral community as such, to other agent-members who can understand our accounts. And always, perhaps most of all, we are answerable to ourselves, even if only in retrospect.

In virtue of their mental capacities, agent-members of the moral community carry the burden not only of moral thinking and questioning, but of moral responsibility. Moral agency generally brings with it certain advantages in interactions with sentient non-agents (i.e., as a trend), but the "power" that comes with the mental capacities is not one to be called upon on a whim. This is surely part of what the Kantian notion of self-legislating agency is about. There are other kinds of power that agents can have and this work has focused heavily on socially constructed power, the kind which, if systematically misused, leads to forms of oppression. (For this reason any kind of social power calls for close moral scrutiny in its functioning, and in fact in its claim to legitimacy in the first place.) Moral agency brings with it moral responsibility and insofar as many of the oppressed retain a fair degree of agency, they retain a fair degree of responsibility. Socially disadvantaged agents retain the obligation that all agents have: to exercise their agency in some meaningful way (although not obsessively). For example, consider Laurence Thomas's call on the oppressed to inform the privileged about the nature of their oppression, without which those advantageously placed to effect change will remain largely oblivious to the need for it.[2]

The Moral Community's Support of Agency

I spoke above of the "burden" of moral agency and even though each agent has some fundamental obligations that must be embraced by the person her/himself (like the obligation to engage in moral exploration and reflection now and again over the long term), the burden of agency should not be one that the person carries alone. I said at the beginning of the chapter that the second concern that motivates my vision of a moral community is the empowerment, development, and support of thoughtful moral agency. A commitment to the moral life brings with it a commitment to moral inquiry, but an environment where discussion occurs, where agents can raise questions with one another, offer their thoughts, express their concerns—in short, an environment where moral questioning and thinking are both the individual agent's and the community's business—offers more support than one where each person is left to the person's own intellectual devices. (We seem to be quite a long way from this still in Western societies, with much of the discussion and exchange being "delegated," e.g., to formal academic institutions or to media like journalistic literature and television programs, etc.)

Also, the moral community's support of thoughtful moral agency requires agents to adopt reasonable attitudes toward the ordinary faults and moral failures of good people, people who are generally benevolent and well intentioned. Good people are not morally perfect, and supporting each other in the moral life is a nonstarter if we cannot "accept" morally imperfect people. Moral fallibility is a shared feature of all agents, both those with and without socially constructed power. Genuine goodwill and general benevolence can exist side by side with no awareness of one's own socialized habits, or indeed those of others, at least the more subtle of them. Also, any tendency to think only of specific actions obscures how they contribute to cumulative patterns formed by multiple agents, patterns that are devastating to the victims. Again, a well-disposed attitude toward those we interact with seems to be simply a matter of well-intentioned sociability and perhaps basic kindness. Few think of their role in social structures that consolidate power and status in ways that marginalize nonmembers of "the group" (discussed in Chapter 5). There are many such phenomena that have special significance in the workings of civilized oppression. Quite a range of the oppressors' actions, habits, and oversights may reasonably be viewed sympathetically by the victims, in that they themselves may often have the same experiences, perform analogous actions, or fail to notice the same types of things. Only their social context blocks the potentially oppressive effects—and sometimes it does not, for example, they can be oppressive to members of other groups. In the case of violent oppression committed by competent adults, it is far more straightforward to see the oppressor as the enemy, the one we need to fight against with all we have. With civilized oppression, many agents lack the usual, striking features of character that mark them as villains. In fact, some contributing agents would enter into physically dangerous situations to rescue another, and some contributing agents are actively striving to diminish the oppression or trying to protect the victims from further harm (as in certain types of "blaming the victim" patterns).[3] It is not true that all oppressors, to quote Ann Cudd, "intend to act in order to continue or intensify the oppression of a social group,"[4] and to actually build this feature into the definition is a breathtaking dismissal of an enormous amount of civilized oppression.

Ordinary people who do much good in the world are imperfect, but "accepting" each other in the sense intended here is neither the same as accepting the moral status quo nor the same as accepting their beliefs and practices. Civilized oppression is sustained by ordinarily good people who are socially well placed, by people who are typically not self-aware (e.g., with respect to their own actions), who do not seriously reflect on the different levels and kinds of social power and how they function, who do not notice the nonviolent subordination they both inflict and often benefit from, nor the social deference they receive throughout their daily lives. But accepting the agents does not mean accepting the oversights. In fact, their moving forward to more informed perception is morally pressing upon them. (What form the "moving forward" should take can vary depending on the situation of the agents in question, but standardly it needs to begin with moral thinking and questioning, and then, other things being equal, move into much sharper perceptions along with changes in action.) There is nothing incompatible in saying that given the subtlety of much of civilized oppression, their initial lack of awareness is understandable and does not in itself indicate a dreadful moral character, but that they nonetheless have an obligation to begin to work on learning about the phenomena and functioning of such oppression. The acceptance of those with initial oversights does not remove the moral call, again shared by all agents, for them to move forward, nor does it mean that they are to be left in blissful ignorance to pursue their daily lives unaware of their contributions to oppression. Indifference to the moral progress of a society is a failure of a moral community, but indifference to such progress does not require any grand, ideological stance. All it needs is a general indifference to individual moral agents, both oneself and others, and their engagement with the moral life. (There is of course a difference between moral imperfection and evil, but I have referred here to people with basically goodwill, and that includes many agents of civilized oppression.)

To see oneself as a member of any community is to see oneself as connected in some way to other members. If relationships of empathetic understanding play a central role, then giving and accepting help is, within reasonable bounds, a natural aspect of community and is neither arrogant for the giver, nor demeaning for the receiver. In particular, it does not in itself signal a paternalistic attitude. As argued in Chapter 2, we need to distinguish high-handed paternalism from the offers of help and assistance that are natural in community. In fact, I think we need to be careful about a blanket condemnation of help given that was not first offered, given both the range of those at the receiving end of oppression (not all have any significant moral agency) and also the kinds of unexpected situations that can arise, even when they do involve, often in absentia, oppressed others who do have moral agency. Although I support a strong sense of "individuality" (which I will say more about in the final chapter), this does not involve trying to move through life independently. As an ideal, even its sheer feasibility is highly suspect, but it also embodies a rejection of any meaningful sense of community. A sense of self is not the same as a strong sense—or illusion—of self-sufficiency. Helping and being helped are both expressions of community.

That is to say, the kind of acceptance and support morally called for in our interactions with generally good people in the moral community is different from simply respecting each others' negative rights to life, liberty, and possessions. Such respect is a moral obligation, but it is not enough. A different form of respect that I will outline in Chapter 5 (to do with a different set of basic rights and obligations, correlated with a basic level of moral endeavor) is also owed, but again, it is not enough. Community is a context where there is a predisposition to be *engaged* with one another, to be in moral solidarity with one another. To be predisposed to try to empathetically understand another is to be predisposed to engage. The notion of a moral community calls for us to live alongside each other in ongoing ways, but also calls for us to think of others as part of the community even when they are not in physical proximity. It is a way of seeing and thinking about others, a way of "responding" to them and their situation, including others never met.

Moral Community and Celebration

I do not share the traditional conception of the moral community, but perhaps in any case I should confess that the traditional notion has always struck me as rather joyless. The agent-members' commitment to the moral life is vital of course (as it is in the community I envisage). For myself, I have found moral exploration often frustrating and sometimes very satisfying, and the ultimately associated obligation to try to make changes, for example, in my actions, the nature of my omissions, in interactions with others, in urging changes at the societal level, and so on, challenging. Yet although only those with agency can undertake these obligations, this does not mean that a moral agent is simply and solely someone committed to the moral life. There is more to the person than this. Agents fall in love, read detective novels, go to food banks, go for walks, take up tennis, apply for new employment, admire the flowers, search for an affordable basement room, watch their parents become frail, take their children to the park, and so on. Many daily life activities are not inherently moral in kind, but they often provide opportunities for achievements or special moments as well as disappointments. And they provide vehicles for aspects of our individuality. Empathetic understanding of others should not be limited to times of hardship or matters to do with the moral aspects of living. It is just as appropriate when another has at last found a job or resolved an estrangement with a relative. And it is not just agents who have special times and special events. Empathetic understanding is appropriate when a rescued, formerly abused dog for the first time walks toward you without hesitation, tail wagging, and trust shown in the very way the head is held and the eyes make contact. Empathetic understanding is, among other things, a source of celebration of others, of the joys and achievements that they may or may not be able to talk about. Community is about affirmation and connectedness, and the "sharing" should bring within its scope more than suffering and more than aspects of the moral life. Moral solidarity centered around such empathetic understanding should prompt not only the pain we feel when the suffering of another becomes "real," but the delight we feel (or should feel) when we begin to grasp the special moments in the lives of others. And this holds for fellow members at great distances from us. When the cure for leprosy was developed, there should have been dancing in the streets across the world. Issues to do with funding the distribution still remained (although I gather that the pharmaceutical company responsible for it has, for many years, made the medication available without cost), but that any such treatment had been produced at all was surely a stunning breakthrough in the thousands of years of appalling physical, social, and personal suffering caused by this disease. That this illness strikes nearly exclusively outside of North America and Europe is irrelevant, unless we see geographical distance from "ourselves" as carrying moral weight, a stance that is saturated with dismaying self-interest. Empathetic understanding as a source of celebration of others and their joys is an aspect of community we are even further away from at this time than the aspect of moral solidarity and response to fellow members who suffer.

Can we be in a relationship of moral solidarity with all members of the moral community? Can we empathize with all of their sources of joy?

I mentioned in an earlier chapter that there might be limits to the reach of empathetic understanding, at least in some forms, and that the distinction between ordinary moral failings and evil is significant. We owe all fellow agents some forms of respect, like treating them with "interactional justice" (explored in a later chapter), regardless of their moral character and the nature of their deeds. Perhaps too some forms of suffering experienced by agents who commit evil also call for at least some empathy. We may not empathize with the imprisonment they suffer, but we may hold a very different attitude and be in a very different relationship with them if they are subjected to systematic torture. We may stand in moral solidarity with all victims of torture, regardless of their actions and moral character. Such forms of connectedness with the truly evil may remain even if the idea of celebrating their special moments seems unreasonable. Celebrating the moments of light in the lives of ordinary fellow members of the community (imperfections notwithstanding and non-agents included), and indeed affirming fellow members in a variety of ways, is, though, a natural expression of the inclusive moral community envisaged here.

The Paradigm of Resisting Oppression

I claim above that in a range of cases, agents who contribute to civilized oppression may be exhibiting failings that all share, including the victims, and that it is appropriate to the sense of moral community to "accept" these agents, even while calling on them to move forward in their perceptions, thinking, and actions. How then should we think of resistance in the case of civilized oppression? Does oppression of this kind rightly affect what resistance should consist of?

Oppression is by definition unjust and to be resisted, but as with a number of other issues, overgeneralizing oppression leads to misleading conclusions, which includes claims about resistance. The nature of civilized oppression and the nature of the moral relations it can involve bring with them significant differences between such situations and those involving violence and/or the use of law when it comes to thinking about resistance. I draw attention here to some of these relevant differences insofar as they affect issues to do with resistance and then look at two nonstandard forms of resistance that are especially relevant to civilized oppression. They speak to the nature of the moral relations that hold (or should hold) in the case of civilized oppression.

When we think of resisting oppression, we think first of events like the rescue of Danish Jews by their fellow citizens when they were about to be deported to death camps in World War II. Over 6,000 were ferried to safety in Sweden. Fewer than 500 were captured. This event displays the features we expect to find in a paradigm case of resistance: the oppressors are clearly "the enemy," in that they clearly intend serious harm, even death, to the victims and cannot reasonably claim to be unaware of this; the resistance involves many people united in a common cause; it is aimed directly at thwarting a violently oppressive action; and it constitutes an act of transparent rebellion against the Nazi regime. It also displays features we first think of as desirable. It succeeded in two key respects: those involved did indeed save thousands of lives and did so in a way that clearly conveyed the defiance of the Danish people for the Nazis and their worldview. The cases we think of as paradigms of resistance are often the dramatic ones, like the example given above.

Such eye-catching cases prompt several plausible beliefs about oppression in general and therefore resistance in general, but there are dangers in generalizing from these situations to ones where less obvious forms of oppression are at work, both with respect to the analysis of oppression and resistance, and also with respect to the moral claims that can plausibly be supported. In fact, "oppression in general" is an uneasy phrase, since oppression takes significantly different forms,[5] some of which pose their own special problems. In this work I am, of course, especially interested in civilized oppression and I will focus primarily on issues to do with victims of civilized oppression and their prima facie obligations to resist. I argue that what seem to be central features in paradigm cases of resisting violent oppression often do not hold here and the nature of such oppression poses special challenges when thinking about resistance.

When resisting violent oppression we aim to be effective in one or both of two ways: either in reducing the oppression and/or in sending a clear message of rebellion to the oppressors. Dramatic cases of resistance have a lot to do with dramatic activism. In her book, *Analyzing Oppression*, Ann Cudd emphasizes this when claiming that

> A person or group resists only when they act in a way that could result in lessening oppression or sending a message of revolt or outrage to someone. My account does not categorize as resistance cases where the only ones witnessing the action are incapable of receiving a message and there is no lessening of oppression.[6]

All oppression is systematic: victims are repeatedly mistreated, whether the oppression is violent or not. The more brutal the oppression, the more securely victims realize that they are being systematically wronged, yet even here victims sometimes excuse their oppressors and blame themselves (e.g., battered spouses). Their accounts reveal a further dimension of oppressive harm, a kind of deep psychological abuse that results in false consciousness, and although understandable given the abuse, their moral accounts are tragically inaccurate.

As already noted earlier in this book, civilized oppression is inherently more difficult to recognize, even by its victims. It is often subtle but pervasive, and unlike violent oppression, there is often nothing conspicuous and involves acts of omission. Unlike law-based oppression, the acts of omission are often not codified in any formal document. Unlike violent and law-based oppression, this sphere of oppression often involves matters that cannot sensibly be made the subject matter of law. The most troubling forms operate in realms of the informal where neither law nor explicit institutional policy can feasibly operate.

Victims themselves can find it difficult to spot. It takes a sharp eye to notice the incidents even though they have an impact. I can recall several conferences decades ago where, when a woman raised a question in the discussion period, the response was always pro forma, whereas if a man raised a concern, there was a thoughtful engagement. This difference occurred at one meeting where both the woman and the man asked the same question, the woman in fact asking the question first.

Spotting incidents of this kind does not readily occur, partly because many victims neither expect nor look for problems to do with exclusion and denigration in their work environment. Even when occasional incidents are noticed, those at the receiving end can find sensible excuses for a long time. The session's speaker was tired, so perhaps his attention drifted when the question was asked the first time. Perhaps this was one of his first conference sessions and he was therefore a bit uneasy. There was quite a lot to the question, so perhaps he needed to hear it a second time to take it all in. And so on. Sensible explanations can hold up for a long time, but not indefinitely. At some point, even the most generous spirited of sharp-eyed victims runs out of plausible excuses and faces the unpleasant task of rethinking the nature of the problem.

There are dozens of such apparently small actions that can, and in cases of nonviolent oppression do, form long-term patterns of exclusion, subordination, and denigration that can have a devastating cumulative impact, not only on the psychological well-being of the victims, but also on their opportunities, life path, and chances of fulfillment in various ventures that involve others. Civilized oppression, then, poses a special challenge, in that apparently trivial acts that often pass under the social radar screen can wreck the lives of those systematically at the receiving end. For the non-oppressed, the perceived triviality is a barrier to taking the claims about oppression seriously, and although civilized oppression covers a spectrum of cases, I have argued earlier that there are many where the initial response of the non-oppressed is understandable. The significance of the actions, the way in which they form patterns of systematic abuse, contempt, exploitation, or dismissal, all of this needs to be learned. As hard as it is in these cases for the victims to perceive what is happening, it is harder still for the non-oppressed.

Educational Initiatives as First Stage Resistance

When members of the oppressed group are arrested in the middle of the night, we want to release them from the prison trucks. If they are being shot in voting lines, we want to send in armed guards to protect them. The first line of attack in thinking about resistance is typically aimed at the blatantly oppressive acts. With civilized oppression, on the other hand, often the first line of "attack" is to get people to notice the persistent but subtle acts of discrimination and their effects on the victims. It is a major task in itself to enable people in general just to see that there is a serious problem. Unlike forms of violent oppression where the agents have no morally reasonable line of justification, some agents of civilized oppression (please note, "some") understandably do not recognize their actions as oppressive. At least, it is understandable in these cases prior to the general and widespread educational initiatives that raise awareness about the mechanisms of civilized oppression, something that cannot be achieved overnight. Over time listeners may come to reflect more on what they see and do, but the very nature of the oppression at work means that making a sincere and firm decision not to be a party to it and to intervene when it occurs is not in itself going to succeed. In some cases, in fact, it has already been pointed out earlier in this book that oppressive agents are completely unaware of a whole range of their own actions; they pass beneath their perceptual radar screen. Being alert to the various manifestations of civilized oppression takes not only goodwill, but also a kind of awareness, and certain perceptual skills. This is one of the significant differences between these forms of oppression and the more vicious kinds and has implications to do with resistance.

If the non-oppressed take time to learn about the phenomena, is this resistance? When the oppressed talk about how the incidents form effective mechanisms of exclusion, exploitation, or subordination, is this resistance? I think so. In *Oppression, Privilege, and Resistance*, the editors, Lisa Heldke and Peg O'Connor, write that "if the analysis of systems of oppression tells us anything, it tells us that there exist many ways to resist—because oppression is not just one thing"[7] and the first "strategy of resistance" they mention is education, both formal and informal.[8] Learning from victims of oppression is an often informal educational mode of undermining future oppression and both the listener and the speaker can be seen as engaged in resistance. In fact, for good reasons (explained above), educational initiatives, both formal and informal, are often the first line of attack here. Because of the difference in the kind of oppression involved, moving in directly on the actual actions has a far greater chance of success in the case of violent oppression (or oppression directly reflected in law) than in the case of civilized oppression, and although perhaps we are not accustomed to thinking of explaining and learning, and so on, as acts of resistance, they are crucial components of attempts to end or lessen civilized oppression. I think it is appropriate to think of them as robust forms of "resistance" in these circumstances.

Educational initiatives of this kind reflect one important aspect of the moral relations between the oppressed and the socially advantaged non-oppressed: morally speaking they should be in the role of empathetic and willing learner about oppression, most especially by learning from the victims.

As difficult as it is for victims to perceive and describe what is involved and what the impact is, articulate and thoughtful victims constitute a special source of knowledge and understanding, especially in the case of these less blatant forms of oppression. Yet this source of understanding is largely untapped, unless the privileged are willing to learn about subtle but serious oppression. Indeed the privileged have an obligation to make the effort to imagine and understand what day-to-day life is like for an oppressed person, but this is no ordinary kind of learning. In chapter 3 on "Moral Solidarity," I refer to Elizabeth Spelman's claim that the privileged should make themselves "apprentices" in learning from the oppressed, and to Laurence Thomas's position that the socially advantaged should show "moral deference" to the disadvantaged and oppressed and learn from them about their oppressive experiences and life-situations.[9] Both speak of the "education" of the socially elite and powerful; that is what "learning from the oppressed" means. And they are surely right about the central and primary role of such learning. Without it, no changes to the social practices, institutions, and individual habits can be expected.

Moral Deference and the Obvious Constraints on the Victims' Prima Facie Obligations

Laurence Thomas speaks of moral deference as "a mode of moral learning which those who have been oppressed are owed in the name of eliminating the very state of their oppression...Indeed, the absence of such learning, the studied refusal to engage in such learning, is one of the very ways in which oppression manifests itself."[10] There are grounds for claiming that the non-oppressed should try to understand what the oppression involves by listening to the victims, not, though, as a matter of intellectual curiosity, but with the empathy owed to those who suffer contempt and injustice. The learning curve for the non-oppressed is steep in the case of nonviolent oppression and understandably the initial response is one of trying to "explain away" one incident after another. This is not surprising given that victims themselves often do the same for a long time before realizing that the relentless pattern cannot reasonably be accounted for that way.

As a separate argument, Thomas points out in another article, "Moral Flourishing in an Unjust World," "either diminished category persons [oppressed persons] must play a role in others coming to understand their specific experiences or there will be precious little understanding of any diminished social category group by persons not belonging to it."[11] Thomas, I think, clearly implies here that the oppressed have an obligation to be involved, something I wish to consider more closely. For example, in the same paper on moral flourishing, he writes that "Diminished social category persons who exempt themselves contribute, if only unwittingly, to the continued existence of an unjust world"[12] and even more bluntly claims that the oppressed "fail to do their part in making this world a better place when in the name of being a victim, they insist on being silent."[13] Victims should speak up, protest, and explain. It is an irreplaceable contribution to lessening oppression.

I agree that victims of oppression have a prima facie moral obligation to actively resist, including taking on such educational initiatives, but care is needed in talking about what this means and what kind of justification can be offered. There are some morally obvious limits on the resistance to be called for from victims. If it is a moral obligation, it is an imperfect rather than a perfect duty.

The most obvious concern is that of personal resources, especially time and energy. Speaking up, explaining problems, time after time, is tiring. Since the relevant, oppressive incidents form an ongoing pattern, taking resistance seriously means an ongoing commitment. Thomas refers poignantly to "the weariness of it all that stems from the feeling that one must speak up because no one else will."[14] Ann Cudd writes that "It is implausible to suggest that resistance to oppression by the oppressed is morally required at all times with respect to all forms of oppression...oppression is such a pervasive condition of one's life that it would be impossible to struggle against all of it at once."[15] It would be unreasonably burdensome on an individual's time and energy to expect almost constant engagement.

Sometimes there are also serious prudential concerns, even in the case of nonviolent oppression. There is always vulnerability when resisting oppression, since systematic power differences are central to the nature of oppression. Also, the forms of power here ex hypothesi do not rely on physical force, which is one reason why these forms of oppression are so recalcitrant. Like nearly all aspects of civilized oppression, they are so often not recognized. The power differences also make speaking about oppressive patterns stressful. However phrased, however calmly explained, it is usually and correctly seen as a kind of protest and resistance, and powerfully placed people would rather not hear protest. It is not something that makes anyone's day. So while some risk has to be undertaken if there is ever to be a more socially just way of living, there may come a point when moral obligation moves into the realm of the supererogatory.

A Less Obvious Moral Constraint on the Victims' Prima Facie Obligations

There is at least one less obvious limit, though, of a morally interesting kind. Suppose for the sake of argument that there are no concerns about time, energy, or risk of retaliation. Under these conditions, if reflective victims are the best source of insight about oppression, and if such injustice should be lessened, do we have enough to ground an obligation on the part of such victims to address relevant incidents when they encounter them? It is an attractive position, in that it accords the victims a privileged position; it recognizes the moral deference (to use Thomas's phrase) owed and calls for their voice to be heard. However, what begins as deference can transform itself into a kind of second-order oppression, not because of the drain on time and energy or risk of retaliation, but because the focus on the oppression can begin to coercively define the person's whole identity.

The claim that oppression damages a person's identity or self-conception is of course nothing new, but the damage that philosophical work on oppression now standardly describes is different from what I have in mind here. In feminist philosophy, for example, attention has been drawn to the harm that results from internalizing the negative conceptions, beliefs, and stereotypes of the oppressors. Sandra Bartky writes, "suppose that I, the object of some [negative] stereotype, believe in it myself…I may then find it difficult to achieve what existentialists call an authentic choice of self, or what some psychologists have regarded as a state of self-actualization."[16] My self-conception is affected and so also my self-development. Relatedly, so too is my self-respect. In *Damaged Identities, Narrative Repair*, Hilde Lindemann Nelson notes that

> Although oppression always damages people's identities by depriving them of opportunity, it frequently also has a second kind of destructive impact. A person's identity is twice damaged by oppression when she internalizes as a self-understanding the hateful or dismissive views that other people have of her. The lesbian mother, the wheelchair-bound worker, the Japanese American might all come to see themselves in the terms reserved by the oppressive institutions of their society for people like them. They then lose, or fail to acquire, self-respect.[17]

This is referred to as "infiltrated consciousness," a wonderfully apt phrase.[18] Psychological oppression, then, is a most painful component of the oppressed's lived experience and a powerful weapon in the hands of the alert oppressor. In Bartky's poignant description, "The psychologically oppressed become their own oppressors; they come to exercise harsh dominion over their own self-esteem."[19] The negative messages are internalized and they distort the person's self-conception and wreck both self-respect (the basic sense of respect for myself as a self or person or individual worthy of the same respect as other individuals) and self-esteem (for the nonmoral attributes of myself I would otherwise value).

This is one of the most painful aspects of belonging to an oppressed group—this and the feeling of powerlessness to do anything about it. The threat to self-identity that I have in mind, however, is different. The most striking difference is that it does not originate in those we think of and refer to as the oppressors. The source of the problem lies with people who genuinely respect the victims, who care about the oppression, and are committed to working against it, and who have an attitude of moral deference toward the victims.

When we think of the oppressed being trapped, constrained, confined, it is usually directly tied to their being oppressed. Their experience "is that the living of one's life is confined and shaped by forces and barriers which are not accidental or occasional and hence avoidable...It is the experience of being caged in."[20] This experience of being trapped can readily rule over someone's heart and mind, and confine thought and vision as much as the oppression confines day-to-day life.

Being oppressed, though, can become a form of tyranny in other ways. In particular, a resisting victim can gradually slide into devoting herself just about entirely to working against the kind of oppression experienced, not because of a fully aware, personal choice (which can happen), but in response to the persistent moral expectations of others, especially non-oppressed but concerned others who have an attitude of moral deference toward the victim. They continually ask her views on situations where such oppression is involved. They repeatedly ask permission to put her name forward as a spokesperson at this or that event or as a member of a relevant group or committee. They refer others to her, encouraging them to speak with her, to ask about the experiences of someone oppressed, and to learn more about what it means. When a situation arises where it seems clear that oppression of the relevant kind is a major factor, they stand back and defer to her, letting her take center stage in responding to the situation since she has the relevant experience and insights. After the situation is resolved, they ask her to explain how it all struck her, what she noticed that they did not, what her responses were, and why she decided upon them. And so on. And so on. Ex hypothesi, all of this is motivated by moral deference.

I mentioned at the beginning of this section that I am supposing, for the sake of argument, that there are no concerns about time, energy, or risk of retaliation. The concern here is not about personal resources or safety, but with saturation of focus. If not freely chosen, it can constitute an extra dimension of oppression, a second-order oppression, so to say. Deference has been transformed into subtle but persistent compulsion, but from the most unexpected of sources, since paradoxically, those most likely to be responsible for this distortion of self-identity are those who value the insights of the victim and are concerned to understand and lessen the oppression. They are full of goodwill and respect, yet much though both are to be treasured, they give none of us 20–20 vision. Supportive, concerned, and non-oppressed individuals may unwittingly urge the victim into actions and commitments that effectively make resisting oppression the one and only goal of any significance in her life. It can involuntarily permeate her whole being. Although it can happen also to non-oppressed resisters, victims of nonviolent oppression are particularly vulnerable, since without their involvement, much of this oppression will not even be visible, let alone understood. Given this vital role, there is an increased temptation, for all the morally right reasons, to transform moral deference into something different.

Dreams and hopes, life-projects and life-pathways, all reasonable in themselves, may be inaccessible to the oppressed. Yet dreams are important even when there is very little chance of their being fulfilled—in fact especially then. This is not some naive assertion that if we hold fast to our dreams, we can *make* them come true. We can try, but we may or may not succeed if they require the fair cooperation of others. But they also matter because in an important sense I do not know a great deal about myself now if I have not been able to reflect quite a lot about who I would be if the freedom and fair opportunity existed.

When someone is indeed hemmed in by unjust constraints on opportunity and access, dreaming does not thereby become a form of self-indulgence unsuited to the moral urgency of the oppressive situation, something that should be set aside in favor of fighting for the cause. Staking a claim to individuality, even if mainly via the resources of the mind, *is* fighting for the cause. Oppressive structures are built around generalized conceptions of the oppressed group's members, around negative images and demeaning beliefs about "them." The stereotypes form lenses through which the individuals are seen, or rather, remain unseen. In resisting oppression, exploring one's individuality is as important as being in solidarity with others who are oppressed. This is not to undermine the essential role of relationships in a person's identity, but reflective, tenacious, and self-originating dreaming, even when there is no reasonable expectation of the aspirations being realized, is also a key component in developing or enhancing self-identity. It's one kind of psychological resistance, and unlike some other forms of resistance (like protesting or explaining the phenomena involved), such dreams resist oppression precisely by turning away from it. The main moral claim I am arguing for here, then, is that someone who is oppressed has no moral obligation, not even a prima facie obligation, to focus on the oppression to the point that it constrains and defines the entire self-identity.

Concerns about Paternalism

This means that some caution is needed in morally deferring to the victims if we are to avoid its functioning coercively on their self-conception. The moral value of such deference depends on such caution and alertness being in place. The distortion into a coercive, second-order oppression requires no malice, no intent to harm, and no visibly hostile acts. Indeed, the distortion itself is very likely to be in the form of civilized oppression, with all the actions appearing insignificant or even apparently reflecting obvious goodwill, all of it imbued with genuine respect, and all of it without any arrogance. This distortion is more than a remote possibility. In fact the number of cases will increase as the general consciousness of the respect owed to victims of oppression grows.

Another reason why the distortion of moral deference is likely to become more frequent is the concern about paternalism, something already raised in the context of moral solidarity in Chapter 3. Feminist philosophers have for decades drawn attention to the prevalence of objectionable paternalism in sexist practices. Men who have not been at the receiving end of systematic subordination quite often take on the role of interpretative expert of unwitnessed encounters between women and (usually, privileged) men, "correcting" the woman's perceptions and reformulating the verbal exchanges. If the man happens to be someone "known" to him, then of course he firmly declares that "he wouldn't say that or mean that or have such an attitude." It is typically forgotten that often the speaker knows the other man primarily by his interactions with himself, another man. In male dominated situations (e.g., certain professional situations), it is not difficult to have extremely limited evidence of a male colleague's encounters with anyone but other men. Even if the man in question is not personally known, the assumptions about standards of behavior, gathered again by how other men treat you, a man, are generalized and blanket assertions about what they would or would not in other contexts, for example, in their encounters with women, are predictable. There is no moral deference shown to the victims since the "evidence" is already gathered, with of course no awareness of its highly selective nature, nor of the relevance of that fact. Only interaction with victims of civilized oppression, undertaken in the right spirit, can change this state of affairs.

This kind of high-handed paternalism is morally objectionable. This said, there are dangers in overemphasizing the concern. This claim was made in Chapter 3, but here I point out that such an overemphasis can give rise to problematic attitudes, and three of them bear directly on resistance to oppression. In the first place, it can cause privileged, non-oppressed people who are genuinely concerned about the oppression to feel reluctant to involve themselves in some forms of resistance (e.g., protest), no matter how patiently they have tried to learn about the phenomena from the victims. They do not want to be guilty of paternalism. This can easily result in the second-order oppression described above where the actual victims are seen as being "on duty" to protest and explain almost constantly and where their public identity and perhaps their self-identity are defined by their role as an oppressed victim.

In the second place it can give a strong impression that fighting against oppression is no one's responsibility but that of the victims themselves, or at the very least, that it is primarily their responsibility. It is one thing to say, as Thomas does, that victims have some obligation to explain and to inform others about the nature of the oppression. It is quite another to claim that the responsibility for ending or lessening that oppression is basically their responsibility. Given the power structures holding between the victims and the oppressors, such a restriction of responsibility is not only a disaster in practical terms, it also sends a pernicious moral message about what our human response to wrongdoing should be.

The third danger of overemphasizing paternalism that bears on issues of resistance is that of creating in oppressed victims an unrecognized attitude of intolerance of imperfection in those who support them in their resistance. Arrogant paternalism is objectionable and embodies a form of disrespect for the victims, but there is a line to be drawn between this and the simple fact that human beings, no matter how well motivated and prepared, will occasionally "get it wrong." This in itself does not establish that paternalism is at work. In practice, though, I have heard this inference made very quickly, something I think is morally dangerous. The best of people will make some mistakes, but if only the privileged non-oppressed who are morally perfect and infallible are suited to be involved in resistance, then indeed the victims must struggle on alone.

If magnified beyond reasonable bounds, legitimate concern about paternalism toward victims of oppression can hinder rather than boost resistance in at least these three ways. A concern about appearing paternalistic can prompt the non-oppressed to step back from leading roles in an oppressive situation (especially if victims are present), which in turn can lead to the kind of distortion of moral deference explained above. It can support the mistaken belief that the responsibility for tackling oppression is primarily that of the victims. And it can make victims too quick to accuse someone of objectionable paternalism if they do take a significant role and make a slip. This in turn can lead to the victims' being further isolated from the genuinely caring, genuinely committed non-oppressed, and will predictably result in less willingness on the part of the non-oppressed to be actively involved in resistance.

Resistance and Moral Relations

It makes a difference whether we see resistance simply as aimed at blocking or lessening acts of oppression, or whether we see resistance as involving something more, namely, the amending and rebuilding of moral relations. There are implications if we see (as I and many others do) a close connection between, on the one hand, issues to do with resisting oppression and, on the other, fundamental moral matters to do with the nature of the moral community we envision and the various moral relations that should be developed and nurtured within it. This includes moral issues of self-respect, one's relationship toward oneself, if you will. Much has been written on the connection between oppression and self-respect.[21] There is, however, another set of moral relations I wish to consider.

In this book, I am particularly concerned with civilized oppression, but here I wish to look especially at one end of the spectrum of cases falling within such oppression. The phenomena at this far end of the spectrum were considered earlier in connection with moral solidarity, where I argued that in *some* circumstances, a victim might justifiably be in a relationship of moral solidarity with an agent who is contributing to civilized oppression.

By definition, civilized oppression involves neither violence nor the use of law, but where it takes its most subtle form, it involves very fine-grained actions indeed and they seem utterly trivial to those not repeatedly at the receiving end. These cases are not rare, but they are the hardest to notice. Small but patterned differences in communication usually play a role, including repeated acts of omission that are particularly difficult to notice. This end of the civilized oppression spectrum can involve everything from glances given or omitted, tone of voice, interruptions of someone else's speaking, turning away when someone approaches, all of these and dozens more can be either isolated events of no significance or they can form part of a pervasive and relentless pattern, the cumulative impact of which can derail lives. None of these kinds of actions can feasibly fall under institutional regulations, let alone state laws, that give explicit directives. The onus comes down to the level of individuals. Only by becoming a lot more aware of our actions can we begin to explore whether there lies behind these patterns some attitude of animosity, denigration, or dismissal.

In these cases, the agents who are systematically marginalizing members of some group are often acting out of socialized habits acquired without intent or reflection. We think of oppressors as people who, to quote Ann Cudd, "intend to act in order to continue or intensify the oppression of a social group,"[22] but agents of *some* kinds of oppression typically have no such intention. They are often warm-hearted and generally benevolent individuals who are aware of and sometimes actively concerned about domination and discrimination of a more visible kind. They have never thought of themselves as oppressors and would be shocked by the description, and yet they are indeed engaged in systematically disadvantaging members of the group in question.

In the cases I have in mind, the oppressors do not fit the usual model. The problem is not simply that they do not understand how what they are doing can have such devastating effects on people's lives and feelings, how what they do can function oppressively. The problem in the cases of interest here is more basic: they are in a literal sense unaware of their actions. They do not know that they routinely glance first at the men in the meeting to see if they have anything to say, before turning to the women. They are unaware that when a woman raises a concern in the meeting, they end eye contact with them, something they do not do when a man speaks. They are unaware that they are far more comfortable chatting with other men than with women and so share with the other men all kinds of useful information and tips. And in case we jump too quickly to blame, it should be said that if we set aside oppression for a moment, it is an everyday phenomenon. We all have habits we are unaware of. We can and should commit ourselves to uncovering them and reflecting on them, but this is a process that takes time and may never be securely "finished." One person tends to repeat sentences when she is nervous, but does not know this. Someone else keeps randomly inserting the word "like" into every other sentence, but does not know why listeners become irritated. Another writes a five-page essay and uses "notwithstanding" six times with no recognition of this word addiction. In the cases of interest here, however, the unperceived habits are not so innocent; they sustain marginalization. However, since they are so far unaware of their actions, they are not yet in a position to reflect on the significance of those actions and their effects. Unlike the more dramatic situations of oppression, then, these oppressors need have no intention to disadvantage those they oppress. They do not recognize themselves as oppressive and, more to the point, understandably so.

We have no innate perceptual skill that enables us to note each and every action of ours. Those we explicitly think about have a decent chance of being seen by us, but habitual actions often pass unregarded, especially if the habits were acquired in the distant past. This commonplace failing lies behind the special cases I am referring to here, the part of the civilized oppression spectrum where the mechanisms of subordination are at their most subtle. Whether or not socialized habits are as innocuous as they are often assumed to be cannot be determined until we first are fully aware of them, and then take time to reflect on them (including speaking with those the habits affect or involve), but certainly appearances can be deceptive. Agents of this kind of oppression need not be in any obvious sense the enemy, even though it is vital that the habits change. In this respect, the situations are very different from the classic instances of resisting violent oppression where the oppressors are clearly malicious, actively hostile, and obviously the enemy.

There have been arguments that attitudes and indeed labels of reproach should be used even when people are unaware that they are oppressive. Probably the most well known is Cheshire Calhoun's in her article, "Responsibility and Reproach."[23] Calhoun temporarily considers the claim that it "[is] possible to make clear that one excuses while simultaneously offering moral correction,"[24] but rejects this approach. She declares that "it does not work in most adult-adult interactions" since it is "likely to be viewed by the recipient either as insulting, because it impugns his status as a normal adult, or arrogant, because it claims privileged moral authority."[25] But the rejection of this approach hinges on the phrase "moral correction," which at least suggests a certain mode of interaction, one that may not be morally appropriate in the cases being discussed. It is a phrase that suggests a mode that is somewhat condescending, as does the term "reproach." But if we change the mode of the interaction, then I am not convinced that excusing while offering some painfully won moral insight is bound to appear arrogant and so provoke hostility. I sympathize with much of what is claimed in Calhoun's article if we are speaking about the more blatant forms of oppression, including the somewhat more visible cases of nonviolent oppression, for example, a man who at home quietly refuses to do any cleaning, cooking, or child care, but the claim that "The logic of moral language dooms any attempt to sustain or convey the obligatoriness of X, while simultaneously excusing most failures to do X,"[26] is over-generalized. There is nothing incoherent in claiming that we have an obligation to acquire far sharper skills of perceptual awareness about our own actions, a vital component of resistance here, and yet that, since this is something that improves gradually over time, one may in the early stages be excusably unaware of some of one's actions and so also of their moral significance.

Resisting the most subtle cases of oppression raises basic questions about what our relationships should be with those whose ordinary human faults happen, in this case, to have fairly devastating effects. Since the faults are shared by humans in general, members of one oppressed group sometimes function oppressively in their treatment of members of another oppressed group because of these faults. The unusual situation of the oppressor here is one of the special features of cases at this end of the spectrum of nonviolent oppression: the goodwill, the general benevolence, but the lack of knowledge about some of his long-term, socialized habits all make him a radically different kind of oppressor from the Nazi commandant rounding up the Danish Jews. As stated in an earlier chapter, in such situations, being firmly against the oppression does not necessarily mean being against the oppressors.

Resistance here may mean building relationships with those who unwittingly contribute to the oppression, rather than taking a more hostile attitude toward them, something that would be fully appropriate in more blatant cases. We may build such relationships with the educational initiatives mentioned earlier in this chapter in mind. We may hope to bring more knowledge and empathetic understanding to the contributing agents. But there is more to the suggestion of such relationships than this. If we see the proposed moral relations as playing central roles in our vision of a moral community and if we view such a community as partly a place where we support each other in our ordinary, shared imperfection and failings, then resistance to oppression can sometimes take such a nonstandard form as forming some kind of relationship with those who, at this far end of the civilized oppression spectrum, are oppressive.

I am not suggesting that such initiatives be undertaken in a spirit of submissive appeasement, but as an exercise of moral agency and membership in the moral community. Calhoun notes that "Reproachful labels...confirm our identities as moral agents,"[27] but so do many other initiatives and responses in our moral relations with others. And if one is not living in despair or constant fear, if thoughtful expression of moral agency has survived the oppression, and if empathetic understanding of simple faults, both one's own and those of others, has not evaporated in the grief of being repeatedly denigrated and excluded, then I think some responsibility as a member of the community, however poorly treated, remains, particularly in these special cases. Moral agency is not the only precious attribute people have, nor even the most precious, nor do I accept it as a necessary condition for membership in the moral community. These are not claims I can argue for here, but all this said, such agency is an invaluable partner of hope, and individual moral agency is an indispensable component in working toward social justice, given the nature and prevalence of subtle but serious forms of oppression. Reflective victims of such oppression constitute a special source of understanding about the phenomena and how they function, and this is at least one reason why they are also key players in moving *this* dysfunctional aspect of the moral community forward into something that better reflects mutual respect and support. Success cannot be ensured, but some attempts to improve our moral relations with others and so also the functioning of the moral community is a reasonable and basic moral commitment that can be called for from all—from agents of oppression, privileged non-oppressors, and victims of oppression whose moral self has not been demolished by their experience.

In conclusion, it is dangerous to generalize about oppression as such. Our findings will be overgeneralized and we will, I think, miss some important insights about the less paradigmatic forms. If we reflect on the full range of oppressive mechanisms and situations and consider especially civilized oppression, then there are good reasons for claiming that resistance can sometimes take nonstandard forms that reflect insights about the moral relations involved. Educational initiatives, especially informal modes, constitute a crucial first line of attack in connection with civilized oppression. The victims themselves are a vital source of such learning, and I agree with Laurence Thomas and others that victims have some prima facie obligation to be involved in furthering awareness of oppression.

I see the victims' obligations as being both more and less than are usually thought of. I have argued that at least at one end of the civilized oppression spectrum, there are agents of oppression who are radically different from the paradigm cases and that victims should try to inform the relationships that hold between themselves and these oppressors, and in this way should try to help amend the condition of the moral community. In these cases I am not recommending taking such initiatives in a spirit of reproach, but as fellow members of the moral community, fellow strugglers, and even with some empathy for the commonly shared failings that lie behind the oppressive acts in these cases. In these circumstances, such moves are indeed forms of resistance, but recommending that victims do this is probably going beyond what is usually thought of as reasonable to ask of victims of oppression.

On the other hand I have added one less obvious moral constraint to those that set morally sound limits on what should be called for from victims. They are not obliged to mold their self-identity so that is centers solely around their identity as a victim of oppression. The constraint on what they should be prepared to do means that the victims' prima facie obligations are not as stringent as we sometimes think.

Resisting oppression, then, can take many different forms, depending on the kind of oppression involved and how it manifests itself. In some cases, resistance can and sometimes should take some nonstandard form that would be morally ill-suited to situations where vicious oppression occurs. Ultimately what grounds the moral claims I make goes beyond an assessment of the actions per se. I anchor them in a conception of the moral relations that should hold between the individuals in the situation, relations that are strikingly different from what is morally called for in cases where violent oppression occurs. If we are thinking about tackling civilized oppression, then changing or reforming the major social institutions, important though it be, will never be enough. The victims as individuals have key roles to play, if they are allowed to. Morally desirable resistance to oppression reaches all the way from the level of the political down to the level of the intensely personal, and this richness of contribution is a natural consequence of the full range of oppressive experiences, the moral relations lying behind them, and the kind of moral community we envision.

CHAPTER 5

The Irreducibly Individual: "Interactional Justice"

A society where we find pervasive forms of oppression has not achieved social justice. In Western societies civilized oppression is still pervasive while inherently difficult to perceive.

Another feature of civilized oppression, one that I turn to explicitly now, is that its very nature leads us to think about individuals in specific situations and interactions (although the relevance of concrete specifics does not mean that moral principles have no bearing). There are irreducibly "individual" contributions to the situations and patterns of civilized oppression. Correlatively there are irreducibly individual contributions involved in a society free of civilized oppression, contributions that are not arrived at by any trickle-down effects of major social institutions. They are some of the constitutive elements of a socially just society (or one where social justice is an ongoing goal) and no perfection of major social institutions can substitute for them. Two such kinds of contributions to a just society are considered in this book, and in this chapter I look at the first, which I call "interactional justice," something very relevant to civilized oppression. Coming to understand interactional justice highlights one way in which irreducibly individual contributions are involved in civilized oppression and in the goal of ending it.

"Irreducibly Individual" Contributions versus "Moral Atomism"

The notion of such "irreducibly individual" contributions is a very different matter from the misguided "moral atomism" referred to in Chapter 2. Moral atomism is a label I use to refer to trying to morally analyze a situation by looking only at the key, individual players, those at center stage who are the eye-catching agents or those individuals obviously on the receiving end of their actions. The minor danger is to overlook the roles of individuals not highly visible, but much involved (like the young, dependent children of the poor and temporarily employed laborer who gives money to the homeless person—in the Chapter 2 example). The bigger danger is that of overlooking altogether the role of social structures, widespread social practices, standard background conditions to do with the economic and educational arrangements and opportunities—or lack of them, societal expectations and the social pressures used to enforce them, the variety of forms of social power, both blatant and barely visible, and more. Thinking about these matters can easily transform our first assessments of a moral situation as we reflect on their influence, especially on often powerless individuals. We cannot come to grips with oppression of any kind without taking stock of how they so often render morally atomistic accounts inadequate and superficial.

On the other hand, when speaking of irreducibly individual contributions to a just, non-oppressive society, I am claiming that as individuals we have crucial roles that cannot be duplicated or replaced by any major social institution, no matter how ideal. Initiatives and commitments of certain kinds have to come from us as individuals. Securing justice cannot be delegated to major social institutions, nor can our individual moral involvement be reduced to supporting such institutions, nor even to taking some central moral principle they embody and adopting it in our personal life (e.g., adopting a principle to donate sizeable amounts of money in order to reduce poverty—as indeed some social institutions may be set up to do).[1] The contributions I argue for are more intrinsically individual, in that they must originate in individuals. A social institution may do a considerable amount to financially assist the poor even if individuals (once taxed) do nothing, but what the individuals contribute in the cases I focus on cannot in principle be passed over to any such institution. Institutions may or may not be able to offer a few kinds of limited support, but they cannot fill the gap if individuals fail to contribute in ways I will explain below. All of this is compatible with rejecting a morally atomistic approach to analyzing moral situations.

In mainstream philosophy, there are at least three strong methodological traditions involving social justice: one is to try to reach insights about social justice by arguing for what social justice would involve if we were starting with a blank slate and organizing a fresh and new society. Second, it is still a dominant tradition to conceive of social justice on the distributive model and, third, to construe justice as all about the major social institutions. Each of these three aspects of this traditional approach make it more difficult than it inherently is to take civilized oppression seriously. In the first place, thinking solely about what a just society *should* be like will not yield the insights about civilized oppression that we need if we are to tackle it. The approach is too coarse grained to come to grips with subtle forms of injustice and the less visible phenomena they involve. Second, while the distributive model of social justice lends itself to talking about inequalities and unfairness in regard to material assets like money, matters to do with relationships are poorly handled on this model. (I will explain the relevance of this below.) And third, construing social justice solely in terms of major social institutions is a "top-down" conception of social justice: if we get the basic social institutions right, then justice will trickle down to individual lives. As important as the basic social institutions are, it remains the case that if we understand the phenomena involved in civilized oppression, we can see that some components of social justice necessarily arise from the "ground up," from individuals and their situations, actions, relationships, and interactions, and from moral considerations that apply directly to them. Social justice is not all about major social institutions and in particular, individuals as such have indispensable contributions to make.

The Distributive Paradigm

The distributive paradigm of social justice underlies most of the oversight about "interactional justice." Distributive justice centers around the model of individuals accumulating benefits. A privileged person in this model is someone who has more than the average share of socially constructed assets. Property issues are bound to loom large here and writers often choose money as an illustrative example; it fits well into the distributive paradigm. This kind of model makes it easy to overlook or underestimate the role of relationships generally within oppression and it largely ignores a crucial type of benefit of the socially advantaged, which I call "relationship power." Their advantages include power over other people in various relationships. When the central issue in justice theory is the just distribution of assets that individuals then accumulate, it is no surprise that wealth becomes the paradigm case. On the other hand, relationships and issues concerning them are not well handled, as Iris Young shows in her critique in *Justice and the Politics of Difference*,[2] since relationships are not the kinds of things that individuals can "collect" or "accumulate." We can, in principle at least, look at how much wealth each has, but looking at each individual—as an individual—cannot, even in principle, tell us what relationships they are embedded in, nor can it tell us what their life-situation is with respect to what I call relationship power (the power they have in their various relationships). Relationships are not things that are accumulated as holdings by an individual; individuals are embedded in various relationships, some involving a number of people, some only one, some more personally close, some less so. Looking at an individual is not going to let us see these relationships and their relevance to the justice of their life-situation and experiences, yet abuse of relationship power is a major source of civilized oppression.

So although the distribution of benefits and burdens is clearly a major component of social justice, I part company with those who take social justice to *mean* distributive justice. And this claimed equivalence is not unusual.[3] Instead of spindling and mutilating the concept of social justice by trying to treat everything, from money and employment through to liberty and self-respect, as a distributable asset, I separate out justice issues that are more crucially to do with relationships. In particular, I argue that there belongs within the scope of justice a set of basic rights and obligations of this kind, more to do with *relationships and interactions* than to do with distribution of assets.

When those speaking about social justice refer to "basic rights," they often have in mind the "three basic rights" of life, liberty, and possessions and the extensive debate about their moral status as negative or positive rights. That is to say, if someone has a right of some kind, what is the nature of the associated obligation that others have? (Are others obliged simply to refrain from certain actions, obliged not to interfere with the right-holder—roughly the core of their "negative duty," which correlates with the right-holder's "negative right"? Or, on the other hand, are others obliged to actually do something, to perform some action—roughly the core of their "positive duty," which correlates with the right-holder's "positive right"? For example, if there is a basic right to life, does that require others simply to refrain from killing or attacking the right-holder, i.e., refraining from taking her life, or are others morally required to actually do things to actively help sustain or save her life?) I do not dispute how important these claimed rights and their moral statuses are, but I do deny that they constitute the only set of rights that can be considered basic in any special sense. I wish to look at an especially basic set of prima facie rights and correlated obligations that are associated with the moral life, or, perhaps better, they are rights and obligations that arise out of a life of moral endeavor undertaken as a member of the moral community.[4] They apply, I believe, to all members of the moral community who have a fair degree of agency, those who are capable of understanding and responding to the obligations they involve. (I will argue later that membership in the moral community is not restricted to those who have such agency, but here I have those members in mind.) The moral life in this sense involves moral inquiry, fallibility, moral fault, accountability, amendment, forgiveness, and so on, and since the rights and obligations are to do with such features of the moral life, they are especially basic. They are very simply grounded in the fabric of the moral life, in the root experiences of those exercising moral agency and they are compatible with a number of different substantive moral theories and fundamental moral principles where those principles would result in differences in more specific moral conclusions about specific moral issues. Blocking these rights is a moral concern in itself and also often underlies more obvious social and economic inequalities, but by considering this set of rights, we can uncover an unsuspected kind of justice that makes moral demands independently of a concern for distributive justice. (In what follows, the rights and obligations are all prima facie.)

The Moral Life and Some Basic Rights and Obligations

A significant moral wrong is by definition something that should never have been and those in the moral community with a fair degree of moral agency are clearly capable of committing such wrongs. They may also be on the receiving end of them; they can be the victims as well as the agents. Part of what it means to say that such moral wrongs should not have happened is to say that it grounds the prima facie right to object or protest and even to call for an amendment of the wrong (where this is possible). Although we first think of the victims in thinking about these responses, such a right is not restricted to the victims, not if we take the notion of a robust moral community seriously. It is part of the very notion of a community of any kind that members are not isolated individuals who should be left to cope with everything that happens to them entirely by themselves. This is particularly true for the victims of moral wrongs. For comembers of any community, to distance themselves from such victims is to undermine any sense of a genuine community, since this notion necessarily involves relationships that, in some way and to some degree or other, bind us together. Non-victim fellow members of the moral community have a right to bear witness to the wrongs, something that is even more basic than a right to remonstrate, intervene, or prevent. All members of the moral community have a right to be concerned about serious wrongs. Given the very nature of what a serious moral wrong is, this is what comembership in the moral community involves (whether or not we personally know the victims). The right of such responses to the wrongs is not restricted to the victims. In fact, a right to protest may sometimes become a prima facie obligation to protest, even as a "bystander," if the victim lacks the capacity or position to protest effectively without suffering further retaliatory harm.[5]

Also, those members of the moral community with moral agency are not only capable of wrongful harm, they also have the ability to inquire and reflect morally, to think ahead about their actions, and to look back on those already performed to see what insights can be learned. Also, one way or another, they are able, should they choose, to learn more about systematic wrong, about oppression in fact, from the oppressed victims (as urged by Thomas's call for moral deference to be shown to the victims and by Spelman's call for the privileged non-oppressed to apprentice themselves to the victims and learn from them). The capacity for moral wrong together with the ability to develop their moral thinking and reflection grounds an ongoing obligation to review, revise, and try to extend their moral understanding. This is not conceived of as an academic exercise, possible only for some privileged "intellectuals" who are institutionally well placed, but as the kind of basic thinking about our own actions, character, and goals that many (at least, those not situated in truly desperate, practical circumstances) are well able to do now and again throughout our lives. It is the basic commitment to reflect and think carefully about such things on occasion.

I am suggesting, then, that other things being equal, the agent members of the moral community have such a basic obligation, and that we therefore have a right to expect such an ongoing reflective approach in fellow agent-members. While reflection and inquiry cannot ensure sound insights, they are vital to any sound moral commitment. Without them, oversights and confusions remain undetected, dangerous oversimplifications are never modified, and pressing moral questions are shunted to the periphery of our attention.

I am, though, speaking of the commitment to the moral life undertaken within the moral community, not as isolated individuals. Our moral reflection can and should benefit from sharing our thoughts with fellow members sometimes, from listening to them (including the oppressed members), to raise questions, queries, and concerns with others, and to expect others to do so with us. Prima facie obligations to consider, listen, pay attention, inquire, and rethink correlate with the right of agents in the moral community to present to one another information and arguments expected to help in our moral inquiry, especially when the presenters have first-hand experience of relevant situations or moral phenomena. Being an agent-member of the moral community does not relieve any of us from obligations to take moral inquiry seriously ourselves, but it does add dimensions and possibilities that allow us collectively to gain further insight from our comembership. Moral inquiry does involve considerable individual effort and commitment, but within the moral community it should not be a solitary or totally private affair.

Actions of moral agents affect others and for this reason at least, agents are accountable for their actions. What is done that affects others is, again, not a private matter, and this grounds an obligation to be reasonably willing to explain the reasons for specific decisions that affect others. It can be seen as something owed to those affected, most especially when exercising power over the less powerful who cannot prevent or undo the decision's impact. Being morally accountable brings with it some implications relevant to oppressive situations. For example, those who are both vulnerable and at the receiving end of these power-backed decisions have the right to hear the justification for those that significantly affect them. This position of course runs counter to much of actual custom, where many fairly powerful agents consider that only those with yet more power, specifically power over *them*, have a right to their justifications. It is what I call an "upward only" accountability. In practice, accountability is routinely selective in Western societies; often the justifications for decisions, explained carefully rather than in some pro forma fashion, are reserved for the socially powerful and this common practice is itself an aspect of civilized oppression.

Even if there are sound reasons why the more powerful agents are making the decision, the more vulnerable, affected fellow members of the moral community have the right to assess these decisions and justifications, and the right to protest them. Indeed, the fact that they are not in a position to make the decisions themselves means there is all the more reason for these rights to be assured. Their lack of practical power does not justify robbing them of the exercise of their moral judgment in matters so close to them. The right to moral assessment, I argue, is a basic right of all members of the moral community who have the relevant abilities. It is an intellectual component of moral autonomy, and in the kind of situation described, it constitutes most of what is left of their autonomy with respect to what could be life-affecting decisions.

For these reasons, the more powerful the agents making the decisions, the more that evasiveness on their part becomes morally dubious.[6]

Several of these rights and obligations remind us that a fair degree of openness and interaction are appropriate in a moral community, for example, some willingness to discuss moral issues and to explain the reasons for one's moral positions and decisions. I think agent-membership in the moral community grounds a few other rights and obligations, like the obligation sometimes to forgive a wrongdoer and support his/her fresh start,[7] but we have enough to work with here.

These rights and obligations help to give shape to what basic moral relations ought to be like. For example, without agreeing on everything that constitutes a serious moral wrong, it still follows that relationships where the more powerful routinely block meaningful protest of any kind from the more vulnerable are violations of the appropriate moral relations. So too are power relations that routinely block information and arguments from the more vulnerable. This is especially pernicious where the input is on first-hand experience only the less powerful have. Also, when the more powerful make decisions that significantly affect the more vulnerable and yet refuse to give any careful justification for their decisions, the basic moral relationships are again distorted.

It is vital to the moral status of agent-members of the moral community that the associated rights and obligations be recognized. Simply checking that, as individuals, they have the usual relevant capacities of such members, that they are able to think, remember, imagine, foresee consequences, and so on, is not enough. One must be able to *function* in certain ways. Certainly some of the "being able" is to do with the individual's own characteristics, but it is a shadowy and insubstantial kind of "being able" if the freedom to function appropriately as a member of the moral community is systematically blocked in serious ways. For an agent-member, genuinely having the moral status that is their due means being situated within the moral community in a web of relationships that sustain the *functioning* moral self with those basic rights (even though some relationships involve a lot more than this). That is to say, the relationships in which one is embedded should enable and even support (among other things) the individual's exercise of these basic prima facie rights and obligations. It constitutes not only one form of moral respect, it is also, given the nature of some of the rights, a form of political acceptance and recognition.

This basic set of rights and obligations are grounded in the nature of the moral life of agent-members of the moral community and yet they clearly involve matters of justice. They are more to do with interactions and the nature of relationships than they are to do with matters of distribution. As mentioned earlier in the chapter, I separate out for analysis justice issues of this kind from those that are squarely matters of distributing benefits or burdens. In fact I am proposing that we conceive of social justice as including both distributive justice and what I call interactional justice, within which belongs the set of rights and obligations that attach to agents in the moral community and to the sound moral relations they imply. (On principle, I am not ruling out the possibility that other sets of rights belong here too.)

Given the role of power differences in oppression of all forms, I wish now to return to the role of power relations in considerations of justice.

A number of philosophers have drawn attention to the causal connections between material assets and power over other people, that is, between straightforwardly distributable benefits and what I call relationship power. Some writers have drawn attention to the possible abuse of relationship power in connection with the distributive paradigm of social justice. Food, shelter, and similar basic survival items are not only important in themselves, but also because having such assets is connected with a kind of basic freedom. On a libertarian position, consent in just about any conditions seems to count as "voluntary," providing that neither physical force nor the threat of it is used, but there are obvious objections to this conception of "voluntariness." One need not use outright force or the threat of force to successfully impose outrageous arrangements on the destitute, given that they may have only the options of dying or "consenting." Few other than libertarians are willing to call such arrangements "voluntary exchanges," even though direct force is not at work. By contrast, positive welfare rights are thought to bring with them some minimal relief from exploitation. If basic welfare is assured as a right, then it seems that at least the worst of such coerced "choices" may be avoided. Some liberals pursue further this connection between the voluntariness of "exchanges" and matters like wealth. Kai Nielsen, for example, sets his sights on something higher than the minimum provision that comes with basic welfare rights, arguing that "Given the way political and economic phenomena interact, liberty and moral autonomy cannot but suffer when there are substantial differences in wealth."[8] He is alert to the causal connections that hold between straightforwardly material assets like wealth (something that can be well handled on the distributive paradigm) and less material kinds of items like liberty and moral autonomy. Such causal connections constitute one reason why he proposes a far more radical egalitarianism than most liberals.

Basic Rights in Interactional Justice:
Positive or Negative Rights?

But I wish now to set aside the distributive component of social justice and say something about the role of power relations within the sphere of interactional justice. Some of the prima facie rights I have argued for above are perhaps straightforwardly "positive rights," for example, the right to hear a justification for power-backed decisions that significantly affect your life. Of course, there is a case to be made for anyone at the receiving end of such a decision hearing the justification, but if there is only so much time and energy to be give to the task of justification, then it is the most vulnerable, the least powerful, of those affected who have first claim here. Those who have more power than the decision makers, or even much the same power, are in a far better position to make contact with the decision makers on their own initiative if they are concerned. The underlying point here surfaces even more noticeably with respect to the right to protest wrongdoing and points to the centrality of power relations in considering the rights and obligations that attach to interactional justice.

On the traditional explanation of what a negative and a positive right is, the right to protest a serious wrong is not a negative right: that others refrain from this or that action, that they not "interfere," is not enough to get protest off the ground. A lone individual carrying a placard in the wilderness is unable to protest unless someone at some time is in a position to take note of the act. Protest is not the same as voicing objections alone in your private room. It necessarily involves more than the protester. Perhaps more often overlooked is that it is, further, not sufficient that someone physically hear or read what is said in the protest. Whether the protest takes a milder form of raising of a concern or involves an indignant confrontation, it is, in one form or another, an interaction between people (or between people and the media, etc.). At the very least, the listener or reader needs to attend to and reflect upon what is said. Biologically "hearing" or "seeing" are not what I am referring to.

This much suggests that the right to protest involves a positive right, that it requires another to do something, since some individual has to listen and also reflect carefully (and sometimes more) before the right is genuinely exercisable by the would-be protester. And if protest is a prima facie right, then someone has a prima facie obligation, a duty, to do so. It may be some specific official in some institution; it may be the state government (its representatives) as such; it may be people who happen to be around and observe some incident; it may be the general public at large. Whose obligation it is cannot be settled in the abstract; we need to know about the situation and the nature of the protest and protester.

All this is true so far as it goes. In fact, the *specific actions of listening carefully and reflecting with an open mind* may be readily forthcoming from the listener if the would-be protester is a peer with respect to social status and power, is someone with a similar social standing and acceptance. Even here this cannot be assured; it remains the case that people in general would rather not hear protests and objections.

The situation, though, tends to be significantly different if the two (or more) key players are non-peers with respect to social status. Those who are less powerful and vulnerable know that protesting can be a risky business. It can bring retaliatory harm to the "trouble-maker." There is often a reasonable reluctance on the part of the would-be protester to voice an objection even when accompanied by reasons for it. When the difference in power is socially supported, there exists an often unquestioned difference in relationship power and the vulnerable in society are very aware that this can be readily misused. The fear of retaliation of some kind is not a psychological failing on the part of the vulnerable, but more often a reflection of experience, whether first hand or not. Consider, for example, both the actual need for legislation to protect whistle blowers (i.e., why should it be so desperately needed?), and the many cases where such legislation has made not the slightest difference as to how the whistle blowers have been treated. Retaliation can take many forms; one does not have to fire someone from her job in order to make her working life such a misery that she must, for her own survival, leave. A truly toxic work environment is every bit as effective as outright dismissal, but if such an environment is created with some skill, then her decision to leave is, it appears, a purely voluntary and personal decision. If retaliation consists of removing someone, then rarely does it require such a blunt instrument as explicit dismissal. And if retaliation involves something not so drastic, then it is even easier to effect while keeping up the appearance of an appropriately functioning workplace. Other types of social situations not explicitly to do with employment also involve socially structured differences in power between the would-be protester and the one (or the group) to whom the protest is made. Retaliation is possible in these types of cases also. Perhaps the coach moves the protesting teen from a favored position on the soccer team to one that is more peripheral. Perhaps he is removed from the team altogether. Perhaps the complaining customer is deliberately passed from one telephone operator to another without reaching anyone who will take her complaint seriously, or perhaps the operator hangs up. Power differences can go awry without a work environment being involved and indeed without the more powerful being explicitly aware that they are indeed utilizing forms of retaliation.

A would-be protester can be discouraged for other understandable reasons also. Anyone with a decent amount of life experience knows that protest is often blocked via the tactic of hearing the person out, but with no intention of genuinely listening to what is said. It is a kind of refusal to engage. How often have we seen meetings supposedly soliciting "public input" on some institutional (often governmental) decision where there is abundant evidence that the decision was settled before the meeting began, that those supposedly listening are in fact distracted, impatient, and totally unwilling to respond in any genuine way to any of the points raised by members of the public? Such meetings can be genuine, but there is plenty of visible evidence that a significant number are not, that they are held precisely in order to satisfy the appearance of public consultation. Meetings of other kinds not involving the public at large can suffer from the same type of corruption, and further, can do so without the more powerful agents explicitly plotting to block protest. Their attitudes carry the day, whether they are aware of them or not. They affect what they do and how they do it, everything from belief that members of the public are completely unqualified to offer any view on the issues to their lack of interest in being at the meeting at all. This tactic is particularly effective over the long term since it drains away the energy, motivation, and courage of those who are trying to raise concerns or objections, and a quite rational (but not inevitable) response is to stop trying after a time. It is not only a futile exercise that wastes both time and energy, it is also a humiliating demonstration of the power. Their lack of importance, the complete safety with which they can be ignored or trivialized, are crystal clear, and it highlights in a fairly depressing fashion their lack of standing and the general lack of respect expressed.

As though these legitimate concerns were not enough to seriously deter protest from the less powerful, often there is additionally a problem in actually making contact with the appropriate person (or group) at all. Again, this is at its worst when there is a major difference in power and status between the protester and the one responding to the protest. Differences in social standing are often correlated with certain building designs, in that the "important" person has a special location away from the hurly burly of lower-level interactions, and the higher the standing, the more inaccessible the location tends to be. Typically in institutional buildings the more important the person, the further anyone will have to walk to locate where she is and the more barriers, the more checks on what you are doing and where you are going, intervene. It makes clear that there is no free access to this person by "just anyone"; potential visitors are screened, often several times, before permission is given or withheld. The relative insignificance of the visitor is publicized in this way and it is to be hoped that if the one wishing to seek an audience with one so elect is actually allowed to, that he will feel duly honored and grateful for the favor. These influential messages carry forward to situations that do not involve buildings and, say, office locations within them. The knowledge that one is seen as prima facie unworthy to disturb either the peace of the business of someone so important is not left at the door when leaving the building. Again, there is no claim that institutional buildings are always structured in these ways and always send such clear messages, but it is quite a common practice. And these strong messages can produce oppressive psychological barriers when trying to approach the more powerful, even when things like building designs do not themselves involve practical barriers.

And this is the main point here: that in the "default" position where no thoughtful and active measures are taken, the janitor who has just lost his job (as he thinks, unfairly) may not be in a reasonable position to exercise a right to protest to the regional MP about the employer's position on some employment policy. For communications of any kind to occur from the unemployed individual, it is typically the MP who will have to think about how to work on the relationship between herself and her unemployed constituents and how to set up opportunities for interaction. They are unlikely to arise otherwise. That the MP has a private willingness to listen carefully to what any of her constituents has to say, whether unemployed or not, and that she would reflect carefully on what was said if some concern was raised are generally not enough for the right of protest to be in practice exercisable by someone with much less power. For reasons given above, they often find it difficult to have access to the more powerful, and difficult to initiate conversations with them—unless, that is, there has been thought given as to how to counteract the role of this power relation.

The right to protest contains a negative right component—that of letting the protester speak or write or demonstrate (even if limited to peaceful demonstrations), but it also contains a positive right component—that of the recipient of the protest genuinely paying attention and reflecting on the content of the protest. In cases involving major power differences, what the positive right component requires if the right to protest is to be genuinely accessible is more than certain specific acts at the time of protest. The specific act of the MP being willing to listen to her unemployed constituents is necessary, but not enough. Having an aide show all visitors to her office is not enough. The pervasive social attitudes and practices remain and their psychological influence and practical effects are strong long before the kinds of specific acts mentioned become relevant. They constitute *background conditions* that for many people function as barriers to their approaching an MP and they need to be changed if the right to protest is to be far more widely exercisable. The changes involve actively building sounder moral relations, and quite possibly actively reforming some specific institutions, even perhaps to rethinking the physical set-up of the buildings and their components. This work would have to be tackled especially on the initiative of the more powerful, since they are the ones better placed to do so. And for every privileged person, or group, the first priority would be the vulnerable who are directly subject to their decisions.

Of course, even with a straightforward positive right like the provision of adequate food for the destitute, one might say the obligation involves more than providing food at the time of need. There may need to be money or food collected earlier so that the supplies are there, in the background, so to speak, ready to distribute. There may need to be the equivalent of food banks strategically placed in the economically poorer parts of town, and so on. But when we focus on our set of basic rights the least powerful have within the sphere of interactional justice, it is the building of appropriate relationships that needs to start ahead of time, relationships that differ from those that are oppressive even while remaining with the sphere of civilized oppression, free of violence. And to some degree this requires active involvement with the vulnerable parties. For example, without explicit and active thought and work, even a genuine willingness to hear concerns often remains unknown. So long as many in prestigious positions remain unwilling, it will take effort for others to let it be known that they, on the other hand, are willing and committed.

In fact, these background conditions for sustaining the basic rights of interactional justice cannot really lie in the background if they are to function as they should. They need to be seen and known, so that the vulnerable can readily function within them and benefit from them. So perhaps I should refer to them as *foreground conditions*. Trying to work toward a moral community where the set of basic moral rights and obligations I have mentioned, those that attach to taking the moral life, are taken seriously, does not mean we can ignore differences in power and status. On the contrary, they affect what the obligations involve for agents variously placed in the social structures and how we secure the exercise of the rights for those differently placed individuals.

Why Interactional Justice Matters

This set of basic rights and obligations gives shape to some of the equally basic moral relations between agent-members of the moral community; it should inform our interactions with others. Too often such interactions are thought of as morally insignificant when visible forms of abuse are absent, but I am arguing that they call for a lot more attention and self-awareness.

There are clearly significant consequences attached to them, especially in oppressive contexts (where power differences are at work). Stifling objections, even queries, is typically easy work for someone with a lot more social power, more relationship power, than the objector. Not everyone so placed will do this and of those who do, many will not explicitly intend to, but it is not difficult to find examples in daily life. Again, if non-victim "observers" are convinced that they have no right to speak up about the wrongs, then in practice, a promising source of amendment, the input from non-victim others, is greatly diminished. I also referred to an obligation for agents to review, revise, and try to extend their moral understanding and to learn about oppression from its victims. Laurence Thomas is surely right when he notes that "either diminished category persons [oppressed persons] must play a role in others coming to understand their specific experiences or there will be precious little understanding of any diminished social category group by persons not belonging to it."[9] The socially advantaged have an obligation to learn from the oppressed and in addition, the oppressed have a prima facie obligation to explain and inform others, especially contributing agents, about what their oppression involves (even though I have already argued that there are several limitations on this obligation). Without the willingness of the privileged to review their thoughts and actions and make changes, diminishing civilized oppression is an unrealizable goal. Informed input from the victims makes an enormous difference. Similarly, when agents see themselves as accountable to others in the moral community, particularly to the more vulnerable over whom they exercise their decision-making power, justifications for those decisions should be forthcoming and this in turn allows for response from those affected and for changes to the decision where appropriate. Given that the focus is on civilized oppression, the actions initially decided upon will not be dramatically awful in any highly noticeable way, so stating the justification for them allows for responses and objections that are fair and informed and that stand a chance of being seen to be so by the decision makers. The exchanges and typically the outcomes of them suffer when the justification is withheld.

There are other less direct consequences of the rights and obligations. Systematic violations of them can have a major impact on straightforwardly distributive issues where material burdens and assets are at stake. Matters of interactional justice (which includes how these rights and obligations function in a society) are quite typically the gateways to any grand design of the distributive kind. For example, there can be a well-intentioned arrangement for the provision of some material benefits to those in dire need, which, however, is not reasonably accessible by those who need it because of some interactional injustice that blocks their access. When the applicants go to the offices to apply, they find most of the personnel scornful and their behavior derogatory. The experience is thoroughly demeaning and they are deeply reluctant to go and apply. If those employed in the offices do not, even in the longer term, learn about the experiences of the very poor in their society, if they carry with them unexamined stereotypes about the destitute and are not open to reviewing their thinking and assumptions, then they fail in what should be a commitment to ordinary moral inquiry, an element of the moral life. Although by no means limited to thinking about those we actually have dealings with, they are surely included within the obligation if those are the ones we are most likely to affect for good or for ill. The distribution of a material benefit may in practice be effected only in ways that constitute assaults on proper moral relations; only, that is, by inflicting interactional injustice on the recipients of that benefit. Some people in serious deprivation of some material kind have forgone such a benefit precisely because of the interactional injustice they must endure in order to receive it. The price of decent food may be moral subordination and the price may be too high.[10]

There are other examples of ways in which the basic rights and obligations have value from a consequentialist position, but throughout this and earlier work, it is a recurring theme that, as precious as good consequences are, there are other morally pressing considerations in matters to do with civilized oppression. That is the case here: interactional justice matters in its own right. It embodies one form of respect that should hold between agent-members of the moral community. Not all members are agents, and the respect that should hold between those who are may not be exhausted by a commitment to interactional justice (more on this later), but it is one important component of that respect.

Many have argued that respect is owed to others who have a fair degree of moral agency, yet when this respect is "cashed out," the kinds of things listed as either duties or appropriate behavior can be rather haphazard. For example, in his discussion of justice and equality, Gregory Vlastos notes that if respect "were applicable *only* in relations of personal love, it would be irrelevant for the analysis of justice,"[11] and refers to "the role of [individuals having] the same value in the moral community."[12] But then he goes on to say that "To be sincere, reliable, fair, kind, tolerant, un-intrusive, modest in my relations with my fellows is not due them because they have made brilliant or even passing moral grades, but simply because they happen to be fellow-members of the moral community."[13] These are surely all elements of ordinary, decent behavior, but citing them as a clarification of the respect owed to other members of the moral community (for myself, other agent-members) involves a confusion between two distinct notions of respect.

Thanks to Stephen Darwall's important paper, "Two Kinds of Respect,"[14] we can distinguish between, on the one hand, "recognition respect"—owed to all "moral persons" (agents in the moral community), regardless of their moral character or actions, and, on the other hand, "appraisal respect," which, as the label implies, is owed only when some-one is judged to be deserving of that respect. It is in that sense "earned," whereas recognition respect is not. Appraisal respect, then, can apply to someone's moral character and it can be higher or lower. Vlastos is clearly referring to recognition-respect, respect that is owed to someone even if they have failing "moral grades" and so deserve very little, if any, appraisal-respect. The position implies that there is a type of respect owed just as much to the sadistic serial murderer as to the selfless individual who conceals a Jewish family from the SS. But, to refer back to Vlastos's examples of what is called for, it is not clear that we do owe the serial mur-derer anything like "reliability" or "kindness" (in any positive sense over and above refraining from cruelty). It is even less clear that we are obliged to be "un-intrusive," and blatantly clear that we have a duty *not* to be "tol-erant." Vlastos's list of the kinds of actions that reflect recognition respect looks plausible only when we think of ordinarily decent people who, like most people, deserve a significant degree of appraisal respect.

The usual move is to insist that the individuals are intrinsically valu-able even if their moral character and their actions are appalling. Vlastos himself speaks of their "intrinsic value as individual human beings,"[15] but it is not easy to ground this intrinsic value. For the moment, I wish to say that even without debating that issue, the set of basic rights and obligations set out above do apply to all moral agents, regardless of their actions and moral character, regardless of any very low appraisal respect, and they embody a type of respect that can and should be afforded to even the worst of moral offenders. Even the serial killer has the right to protest an action he believes to be unjust, to hear the justification for decisions taken about him, to expect others, for example, those involved in any legal action against him, to be reflective and thoughtful and pre-pared to modify or change their views if appropriate, He also has obliga-tions, including that of holding himself accountable for his actions. The basic rights and obligations argued for make no pretense to be solely for each individual's benefit or comfort. They constitute at least one form of recognition respect and their standing is not dependent on the appraisal respect owed to any individual. If they are, as I argue, applicable at least to all moral agents, then their grounding lies in the nature of the moral life rather than in claims about the intrinsic value of each and every moral agent.[16]

If this set of rights and obligations does constitute a form of recognition respect, then it confers a value that is nonconsequentialist in kind. The rights and obligations matter morally regardless of their consequences. In that case, interactions not involving anything like violence or blatant abuse are nonetheless open to moral scrutiny and calls for amendment. Violations are morally inappropriate and unfair, involving types of discrimination where none is justifiable. Interactional justice—and injustice—matter in their own right, distinct from their often-oppressive consequences.

The Irreducibly Individual in Interactional Justice

No government and no other more bounded institution can regulate anything but the most blatant kinds of interactional injustice. There can be laws about killing others, attacking them, stealing from them, passing off fraudulent credentials, and so on, but there can be neither state laws nor institutional regulations about turning away from someone whenever he speaks, or giving only a pro forma justification for a decision, or refusing to actually listen to members of the public speaking in a "consultative" meeting. When interactional justice is violated within the realm of civilized oppression, it involves such violations, and the actions are rarely open to explicit and publicly established confirmation and condemnation. As so often with this kind of oppression, they are by their very nature too subtle for such a process. Yet they matter morally, both for consequentialist and nonconsequentialist reasons.

Interactional justice constitutes a crucial component of a non-oppressed life-situation, but injustice here is something encountered repeatedly by victims of civilized oppression, and usually without recourse in their own right, given their relative lack of socially constructed power. If we reject the common assumptions that social justice is synonymous with distribute justice, that it is all about major social institutions on the grand scale and the distribution of benefits and burdens that result from them, if we reject the view that social justice is a top-down affair where justice somehow trickles down from these institutions, then it is quite consistent to claim, as I do, that interactions of subtle kind are both a matter of social justice (constituting what I call interactional justice) and also a matter of one kind of moral respect.

And for reasons given, I do reject these common assumptions. For example, when Brian Barry speaks of being "concerned with justice in its wholesale rather than its retail form—with institutions rather than individual outcomes," he gives what is an attractive, but misleading metaphor.[17] If "justice retail" refers to individual outcomes and interactions, and is taken to follow empirically from "justice wholesale," then we have misjudged the place within a theory of social justice of some sets of outcomes and interactions.

The interactional justice component of social justice is different in kind and indispensable and it arises from the ground up, not from the top down. In its nonviolent forms, it cannot be safely arrived at as some top-down effect from major social institutions. The moral community underlies the whole fabric of society; it is not functionally distinct from it. Its functioning is critical with respect to social justice and some of its functioning neither empirically follows from the nature of the major social institutions nor can it be regulated by them. It is inherently insufficiently blatant and dramatic to be so regulated and yet that in no way means it is either empirically ineffective or morally trivial.

The moral community (or those in it) can function badly and violations of the moral relations that should hold in our interactions play a central role in the life experience of many. Interactions between individuals—not involving violence—make up one of the primary sites for civilized oppression when the individuals involved differ in status and social power. And within a whole range of cases falling within civilized oppression, the interactions pass under most people's moral radar screen. These violations of moral relations matter, again, both empirically (because of their consequences) and morally (because of the disrespect they embody). They reflect morally distorted relationships—and relationships are at the heart of civilized oppression.

As noted above, this kind of injustice is too fine grained to be blocked via explicit and external regulations, whether state laws or the policies of specific institutions (even though what is going wrong has striking effects on those on the receiving end). I speak of interactional injustice— in its less blatant forms—as essentially arising from the ground up and its amendment can be achieved only from the same orientation. Individuals as individuals are the ones who have to become sufficiently self-aware to be able to reflect on their interactions with others, even in cases where onlookers will predictably not give the interaction a second glance. There are forms of relationship power that the socially advantaged have in abundance, often without realizing it, and much of it can readily be misused in interactions. For example, in an earlier work I referred to "interactive power":

> Roughly, it is the power to take the initiative in a relationship: in beginning and ending a relationship, in insisting on its being modified, and in taking a number of communication initiatives like the power to begin or end a specific contact (like a conversation), to insist on being listened to and on being given answers to reasonable and pertinent questions.[18]

It is quite usual for those with social prestige to be in control of conversations in these ways and few observers will notice the patterns, let alone be concerned about them. Perhaps they will if there is yelling or swearing or a fist slammed on a desk, but not otherwise, not ordinarily. This socially constructed interactive power when applied to communication situations easily enables the privileged to violate the rights of the less advantaged individual; it provides protection when the obligations argued for earlier are not met. She declines to justify a decision, she calmly interrupts the less socially powerful person when some form of protest is attempted, she refuses to respond to requests for reasonable information, she draws the conversation to a close and leaves when it becomes inconvenient to continue. And she does not have to be in any institutional role for these patterns of interactions to occur. Any habits of calling upon interactive power in order to control communicative interactions (whether called upon intentionally or not) tend to extend to situations when the person is not in that institutional role. That is a danger with strong habits.

Interactional injustice is a pervasive component of civilized oppression. By its very nature, initiatives have to be taken by individuals as such, if the distorted moral relations in these situations are to change. That is to say, contributions to these amendments have to come from the ground up. Since interactional justice is grounded far more in the nature of the moral relations that should hold between individuals than it is in the idea of distributing assets, it is a component of social justice separate from the component of genuinely distributive justice. If we are to conceive of a society free from civilized oppression, then we need to reflect on this component, on the nature of our moral relations with each other, and on the irreducibly individual contributions interactional justice calls for.

CHAPTER 6

The Irreducibly Individual: Authentic Social Justice

This chapter examines a second way in which irreducibly individual contributions play a key role in civilized oppression and, correlatively, in a socially just society or one where we aim to radically reduce civilized oppression. Here it is not interactions between individuals that are involved, but the mental lives of individuals. I argued in Chapter 5 that more than major social institutions are involved in social justice, that individuals as such play an irreplaceable role in a non-oppressed society and have indispensable contributions to make in bringing about social justice. I focused in particular on interactions and the fine-grained actions often involved, some of which display patterns that reflect distorted moral relations between those involved. Here I move beyond actions to thinking about the mental lives of agent-members of the moral community and the relevance to a robust conception of a socially just society.

If we are to gain insights about social justice, we need to think carefully about injustice, and as has already been made clear, it comes in different forms. Unless we study the various manifestations of injustice, the conception of a perfectly just society is likely to embody oversights and so not function soundly even as a distant goal to be aimed for. Thomas Simon in his book, *Democracy and Social Injustice*, claims that "injustice can take priority over justice" and mentions several different senses that can be given to this "priority."[1] One sense he calls "moral priority": he writes that, "Without a clear sense of injustice, justice operates in a vacuum."[2] We need to be as insightful about what we need to avoid as we are about what we should be aiming for. He is concerned that "Rawls and other political theorists have the sequence backwards, by starting with principles of justice and leaving injustice largely unarticulated…The notion of suffering plays a peripheral role in Rawls' system. A theory of injustice [Simon's goal] places a fully articulated sense of suffering at the center of the theory."[3] I am sympathetic to Simon's focus and his concerns. We cannot dispense with the need to think about what a socially just society would involve, but such a conception has to be informed by insights gained by studying different forms of injustice. The interplay between developing a conception of social justice and studying actual injustice requires far more input from the latter than is sometimes acknowledged, if, at least, the experience of the oppressed is to take its rightful role in moving the work forward.

In thinking about civilized oppression we should think not only about the victims' suffering; we need to distinguish what I call "authentic social justice" from illusory manifestations. I hope to show that civilized oppression grounds a conception of authentic social justice, not as simply a curious phrase of passing interest, but as something that gives voice to a morally robust sense of social justice, something that anchors social justice as much in the moral life of individuals as it does in the functioning of major social institutions. It points to a second way in which justice calls for irreducibly individual contributions (over and above those required for interactional justice).

Furthermore, there are connections between this notion of authentic social justice and some moral claims about privacy. In particular, it challenges a standardly claimed right to privacy, namely, privacy with respect to the workings of the mind. At least, it challenges the usual understanding of such a right. I will begin by looking briefly at this familiar moral claim about privacy.

Privacy and the Mind

There is of course no one distinction between the public and the private. Nonarbitrary sense can be given to the distinction in a number of different contexts, for a number of different purposes, and with a number of different moral issues taking center stage. In most Western societies, at least, feminist philosophers have waged a fairly effective theoretical war against the use of the public-private distinction to rationalize gender inequality and gender roles that kept women and children trapped and vulnerable in the "private, domestic sphere," under the state-backed power of the male "head of the household."[4] There are other contexts, though, where the distinction is drawn differently, is far less objectionable than the one above, targeted by feminists, and where claims about a moral right to privacy are widely received.

Liberalism in its paradigmatic forms is deeply concerned with liberty and with protecting the individual and "the private life" from inappropriate control and intrusion. In most European societies there is a long history of monarchs imprisoning, torturing, and killing subjects at will, in many cases with no pretense to any judicial process, however imperfect, and no meaningful involvement of the considered judgment of reflective others. Likewise property has been seized from their subjects, again, at will, either by direct appropriation or by unilaterally determined and onerous taxes. Not surprisingly, the traditional negative rights of life, liberty, and property have loomed large in the battle for individual liberty: being subject to arbitrary seizure, torture, and death, whether in your own person or that of your loved ones, fixes the attention. Only with the stronger and more effective curbs on both sovereign and government prerogatives does the collective attention move on to the next most pressing threat to liberty, which is perhaps the "tyranny of the majority," to use Mill's phrase.[5] Even those who rightly critique the problems of the "negative rights only" approach to liberty in many contexts (e.g., with respect to poverty, the institution of the family, access to education and medical care) seem to become rather more sympathetic the further into the "private sphere" the topic of discussion moves. Although the morality of free speech is under renewed moral scrutiny (e.g., in connection with pornography, Holocaust denials, and "hate speech" generally, and parents' "rights" to raise their children as white supremacists), if we take one step further, we reach what I describe as the far reaches of the private sphere, namely, the inner realm of the mind divorced from speech and action.

If there is one sphere of life where claims about a right to privacy are usually received with sympathy, it is the inner world of thoughts, ideas, desires, and conscience. As Paul Fairfield claims in his book, *Public/Private*, "One of liberalism's most celebrated causes, in both its classical and its contemporary manifestation, is to defend individual judgment and conscience against aggressive majorities and the state apparatus at its command."[6] This claimed right to privacy is widely supported and is the most relevant to this chapter.

Tyrannical governments have routinely attempted to form, monitor, and control not only the actions but also the mental life of their citizens. The violence used against citizens who challenge such a government is but one component in the dictator's system of control. No dictator with any acumen tries to control the nation's people by reactive measures alone. The ultimate goal is to stamp out challenge at its source by eradicating the rebellious thoughts that undermine the dictator's power, rather than simply wait until the thoughts find expression in activism, which then has to be squashed. Major institutions such as the media, the educational system, the family, and the psychiatric profession are co-opted for this purpose of stopping protest and reform at its source. In fact, any dictator who has to resort to violence as a matter of routine is basically incompetent.

Tussman and the Government's Responsibility

So concerned are we about the danger of governments controlling mental lives that the predictable response is a vigorous and sweeping claim that the government, whether dictatorial or democratic, has no business in affairs of the mind. We claim a moral right to freedom of thought and conscience as the ultimate sphere of rightful privacy. In describing this commonsense position, Joseph Tussman, in his book, *Government and the Mind*, writes that

> Words and gestures are public; what I think, what I really think, offers itself as the clear case of what is private. So, as private, the mind lies beyond the reach or jurisdiction of public authority. Government may take notice only of the outer persona, of acts, not of thoughts...Public

authority is unlicensed in the private world. It must leave the mind alone.[7]

Actions are "public" and subject to scrutiny and control, but the inner world of the mind is utterly "private" and therefore entirely within the individual's sphere of autonomy and liberty. In a socially just society, then, the moral right to privacy in this, the furthest reaches of the private sphere, will be recognized and respected as a moral obligation. Presumably it will also be reflected in law.

This sensible position is actually one that Tussman rejects. He first cites an often-heard principle that receives a great deal of general support: "What else is the final tyranny than the intrusion into the sphere of the intellect and spirit, into the realm, as I shall call it, of the mind?" but he promptly goes on to declare that he intends to "oppose this mistaken principle and to establish not only that government has authority in the realm of mind, but also that its responsibilities there are among the most important that it has."[8] Tussman himself speaks of the immediate hostility these claims provoke in his audiences, the immediate charges of being in favor of brainwashing or against freedom of speech or hostile to academic freedom or against democracy.[9] The hostile reaction reveals how frequently it is assumed that any government involvement must be bluntly coercive (and therefore morally objectionable here). The assumption is that if coercion is not morally appropriate in connection with the mind, then it means there should be no government involvement at all. It is the image of government as the epitome of coercive power; but there is more to government than this, or at least there should be if we are speaking about a democratic government.[10] In fact, one of Tussman's prime examples of the government's responsibility in matters of the mind is public education, for example, the public school system. That the government is authorized, indeed responsible, for exercising its "teaching power" (his own phrase), and in this way authorized to play a major role in the mental development of its citizens, does not mean introducing indoctrination or brainwashing into the educational system. It does mean, according to Tussman, that the state has both a moral entitlement and a responsibility to initiate and supervise the kind of education the youth of the nation receives.[11] Educational initiatives do not have to involve indoctrination or brainwashing to enhance a generally democratic commitment in a nation's citizens.

If we ask Tussman what anchors this responsibility, he gives a consequentialist response. He reminds us of the simple fact that thoughts, feelings, and beliefs may be private mental states, but they "spill out into conduct that affects others," which makes the mind "a matter of deep public consequence."[12] His appeal to consequentialist significance as the foundation for moral concern is clear in a number of places in the book. The nature and goals of the public school system have major consequences for the society at large.

I will argue that there is more to the political significance of private mental states than this consequentialist concern of Tussman's, but before doing so it should be acknowledged that even this brief mention of Tussman alerts us to two common dangers in thinking about privacy issues.

First, some familiar and "obviously justified" moral claims about privacy and the mind are not at all obvious once they are unpacked. Although it is not my purpose here to examine Tussman's arguments, those he gives for a government's having justified "teaching power" are plausible and so claims about the obvious immorality of any government involvement in the mental lives of its citizens are not at all obvious. Arguing for the government's involvement loses its shock value once we take the time to understand Tussman's position. It challenges the predictable, but oversimplified, objections voiced by those in Tussman's audiences, those who were morally incensed at the very idea that a government could have any legitimate role in the mental lives of its citizens.

Second, discussions of moral rights to privacy are hindered by unsupported assumptions, oversimplifications, and a lack of clarity about the key components, all of which are commonplace in many daily-life discussions. For example, what is meant by the right to privacy in the context in question? In particular, what really does it morally entitle the right-holder to? What are the boundaries of this privacy and what does it block that would otherwise occur? If these things are left unclear, then both the sense of entitlement and the extent of it easily mushroom to form an exaggerated and morally implausible conception of the right to privacy, and when this happens, the sense of violation is all the more easily triggered and usually vociferously expressed. Historically this has occurred with the privacy aspects of freedom of speech. Even now many people think of it as an unbounded right, an unrestricted moral entitlement to say anything, anywhere, at any time, to anyone. It is thought of as a moral right that cannot be overridden by some other, more urgent moral requirement. Were this so, some principle about free speech would function as a kind of fundamental moral principle in ethics, one that allows for no exceptions in its application. Other principles, no matter what their subject matter (e.g., murder, manslaughter, theft, torture, negligence causing death) would then be secondary to it and logically would have to be overridden in conflict situations. Prioritizing freedom of speech to that extent is morally implausible. (Traditionally libel and slander have been seen as grounds for rejecting any exception-free law of free speech, and more recently debates about "hate speech" and pornography have grounded other challenges.) It remains the case, however, that even free speech, which is an act, not a purely mental event, is thought of by many at a prerogative attached to the right of free thought.

These two dangers—about "obvious" points that turn out not to be and about the nature of the privacy being discussed—hold, I think, for the claim I make about the privacy of the mind and its connection with civilized oppression.

The Consequentialist Significance of Thoughts and Attitudes

On what grounds can we claim that beliefs, ideas, thoughts, and attitudes matter morally and in particular, matter for social justice concerns? The most obvious reason is that such workings of the mind matter morally because of their consequences. Thoughts inform beliefs and they in turn influence action. Many of these resulting actions affect others in various ways. Throughout his book, Tussman is concerned about the results of the workings of our minds; there are strong consequentialist reasons for claiming that our mental lives are not morally irrelevant. Where the beliefs and attitudes are shared by many in society and where they are prejudiced and discriminatory, they constitute the driving force behind oppressive action. Resulting actions target and demean members of particular groups solely because they are members of those groups. These actions are no longer simply individual failings on the part of the agents. The fact that so many agents are involved itself means that the actions form social structures of a powerful kind, structures of control, systematic marginalization, exploitation, dismissal, and other forms of disadvantage or rejection.

Given my current interests, I am thinking of actions where no violence (or the use of law) is involved; I am thinking of actions that oppress the vulnerable members of the targeted groups in ways that constitute civilized oppression. The actions follow naturally from the agents' ideas and beliefs. Many of the actions are not intentional, but neither are they accidental. They embody strong patterns, but there is no assurance that these regularities will be perceived by the agents (nor, indeed, by many of the victims, at least initially). As we have noted a number of times, even though the actions are systematic, their nature makes them difficult to be noticed, let alone taken seriously. Yet they are oppressive.

The Non-Consequentialist Significance of Thoughts and Attitudes

So the mind matters here, since it can result in serious but hard-to-spot patterns of acts that function oppressively. The thoughts and attitudes that lie behind these acts have a great deal of causal efficacy. However, I am making a further argument by claiming that the underlying mental workings have a moral and political significance in their own right, not simply as a source of consequentialist concern.

To get at the key point, conceive of the following: there is a situation where questions of fairness or justice are legitimate and where, for everyone in that situation, every action is as it should be. For the sake of this thought experiment ex hypothesi, not only are the big ticket items as they should be, but insofar as legitimate concern applies to very small items, then here too every hand gesture, tone of voice, every word spoken—or not spoken—every glance, every act of omission, are all as they should be. Conceive also of underlying attitudes and beliefs that are at odds with the actions, attitudes that are racist, sexist, classist, or in some other way oppressive. In practice, it would be very difficult for people to hold these attitudes and not have them show in their actions, although, this said, there are individuals who for many years play a role where their actions and beliefs are completely at odds (e.g., in the role of a spy or counteragent or undercover infiltrator). Then I am suggesting that even though the attitudes are not expressed overtly, not in actions, tone of voice, facial expression, or anything else, they are nonetheless of political, not only moral, concern.

Even just this basic claim will provoke an immediate and very strong defense of a right to privacy. If every act of mine is just as it should be, every act of commission and omission, every act big or small, then typically there is indignation at the idea that the inner workings of my mind are anyone's business but mine (except perhaps in a few very special situations like a family setting). Whatever is happening in the mind, there are no untoward consequences that affect others. What others are entitled to with respect to social justice is to be treated fairly, including receiving their fair share of distributable assets (whatever a "fair share" amounts to). That is secured here and they have no further claim on others outside, perhaps, of some special relationships like those of parent-to-child or a spousal relationship.

The right to privacy in regard to the inner working of one's own mind where it does not result in actions that affect others is, I think, the context in which the strongest privacy claim, what seems to be the most morally secure privacy claim, is made. Intrusion into the freedom of the mind here is "the final tyranny." We can expect the usual vociferous kind of objection. "No one has any right to try to form my beliefs or ideas, or change them, or expose or monitor them, or penalize me for them. Since all my actions are morally sound, no one has the moral right to harass me about my beliefs and mental attitudes or even question me about them. In these circumstances I am not answerable or accountable to anyone for my strictly inner beliefs and attitudes. They are no one's business but my own. I am accountable only for my actions." In short, this hypothetical situation provides what is probably the strongest context for claiming that others should (to use Tussman's words) leave my mind alone!

It sounds very sensible, but I think we have here a danger already mentioned: what seems like an obvious moral claim about privacy is not as obvious as it first seems. I believe it inflates what a right to privacy involves and in particular, it exaggerates what "the right-holder" is morally entitled to.

I reject the sweeping moral claims made in this objection. The first important thing to notice is that the objection refers only to two kinds of items: mental beliefs/attitudes on the one hand, and actions on the other. Only these two categories are specified as relevant. This restriction, this dichotomy, is what makes the objection seem so plausible. There is no mention of relationships. The mainstream view of social justice still predominantly equates it with distributive justice and has as the subject matter major social institutions. Yet I have argued that this is an incomplete account, since it cannot handle satisfactorily issues to do with relationships where those issues are pertinent to social justice. The role of relationships in oppression is most striking in the case of civilized oppression rather than in cases of violent oppression. In the latter context, the terrible actions themselves understandably demand so much of our moral attention that we are fully engaged without reaching further into the nature of the relationships behind them. In the case of civilized oppression, the relationships and their distortions are typically central to what is wrong and why it constitutes a form of oppression. Interactional injustice, for example, is to do with distorted moral relations between people, a failure of a kind of basic respect. The specific obligations that are violated are associated with the moral life of agents shared in community, that is, they are very much to do with relationships.

Relationships involve actions, of course, but they are not a matter of actions alone. Attitudes play a key role too, that is, the mental life of those in the relationship also matters. I proposed a thought experiment where a situation involving issues of fairness, where everyone's actions, big and small, are as they should be, but where the attitudes are quite contrary to what the actions indicate. To refine the hypothetical example, suppose a man of color, Sam, is hired for an academic position. Although clearly the most qualified and experienced applicant with respect to teaching, research, and academic service, the committee does not want to recommend him for the position and does not want him in "their" department. The committee members finally decide to shortlist him and later send Sam's name forward, but only out of fear of the repercussions if they do not. They had hoped he would fail in the interview, but he was outstanding, something witnessed by a number of people outside of the department. They know that the administration imposed serious penalties on another department a few years earlier where a case of racism was clearly involved in the hiring process. So, faced for the first time with a superior applicant they do not wish to hire (because he is a man of color), the committee members recommend his hire. They are deeply resentful, but Sam is transparently the best applicant. Again, to highlight what I want to focus on, imagine that ex hypothesi when he arrives and for years afterward, every action, big and small, of all of Sam's departmental colleagues, is what it should be, although offline all of this is motivated by fear-driven self-interest. (In practice, someone would slip up, but it is conceivable and it will point to something important.) The racist beliefs and attitudes remain intact. So does the burning resentment at having to hire him. Sam comes up for annual review and the review letter points to a few things that will improve his chances of receiving tenure. (The thinking is, "We have to keep the right paper trail! If he doesn't get tenure, we don't want him to have an 'out,' just because the usual pointers weren't given.") He seeks advice from a senior colleague on a teaching issue and receives one or two tips (since he could not see how to simply stare Sam down when asked about this). His colleague resents spending his time on this and sees Sam as weak and incompetent, but again is wary of launching into an honest viewpoint. Sam shares something in confidence with the Chair, an incident where a student became abusive in class. The confidence is not violated, but the Chair privately relishes the embarrassing event she now knows about and has nothing but scorn for Sam's part in it. And so it goes on. In short, the actions may *in a sense* be right, but the relationships are terribly wrong.

It is not that in every single instance the attitudes and beliefs must be morally appropriate. In sound, longer-term relationships, there is room for one of the player's having "a bad day." Colleagues and even the best of friends can sometimes have a passing thought that is unfair or unkind, and usually they are not significant enough to transform the soundness of the relationship. If the thought is voiced, it will probably cause the listener to be irritated or angry for a few days, but far less likely to bring about a collapse of the relationship altogether (especially if the offender finds a way, however circuitous, to refer back to the incident with even a hint of regret). Someone can still be reliable, trustworthy, supportive, and empathetic and still have such a lapse once in a rare while. Sound, longer-term relationships can have a fair degree of resilience. After all, a morally sound relationship is not the same as a morally perfect relationship. Good colleagues and good friends are only human, all said and done.

But in Sam's case, the most modest of morally appropriate relationships involved in a fair workplace environment are not there: he is not accepted, not respected, not valued, not known, and there is zero empathy cast in his direction. On the contrary, he is secretly scorned, despised, resented, and every difficulty he faces is a source of glee. Although not deeply personal relationships, collegial relationships involve some attitudinal commitments, and here those commitments are replaced by hostile and disrespectful attitudes. The apparent relationships of respectful collegiality are illusory and deceptive. In describing the situation, I used the word "colleague" here and there, but in fact, given the actual situation, the term has no purchase. Whether or not Sam is a colleague to others in the department, the others fail to be colleagues to Sam. The relationships are not what they seem to be. Everything that Sam does is done under a hostile gaze. Those around him are waiting for him to fail and wanting him to do so. Even with professional relationships, there is a need for basic trust and Sam trusts his "colleagues" while being secretly mocked.

Describing Actions at Different Levels

Are the actions "right" so far as justice is concerned? I said above that the actions may be *in a sense* right, and it will be objected that regardless of the private workings of the mind, all the goods of the relationship are therefore delivered. But caution is needed here, both because of the consequentialist limitation of the objection and because its plausibility depends at which level we describe the actions. For example, to say that someone "extends her sympathy to him in his time of grief and loss," it is not enough that she goes to him, looks "kindly" on him and says that she "has heard of his loss and is sorry to hear of it" if, in fact, she is so malicious that inside she is savoring his misery. It may be an accurate description of the visible "actions," but it is not enough to count as "extending her sympathy to him," since in this unusual case she has no sympathy to extend. The apparent expression of sympathy is deceptive and inauthentic.

In the case of Sam, the right words are said, the right words are written on the annual review forms, the right gestures, facial expressions, tone of voice, and so on are all in place. If we stay with this fairly basic level of description and restrict ourselves to behavioral, attitude-neutral descriptions, then the actions appear right. Furthermore, Sam is content in his work environment. He has no reason not to be. Yet something is morally wrong with both of these situations.

I mentioned earlier in the chapter Thomas Simon's claim that a fully articulated sense of suffering should lie at the center of accounts of injustice, and certainly suffering is often an indicator of injustice. But there is more to injustice than suffering, as pervasive as such experience is. Injustice is often, but not always, felt. Within civilized oppression, victims often need time to become aware that things are not as they should be, let alone become aware of what it is that is wrong. If a woman is raised in an affluent environment relatively separate from the rest of society, with little by way of education or opportunities for open inquiry and discussion, if she is raised to believe that her sole source of fulfillment and happiness is to move from the role of dutiful daughter to dutiful, young married woman to a man of her parents' choosing, then in such a family setting this path may well bring with it considerable contentment (e.g., financial security, a future should her parents be lost, the [expected, at any rate] satisfaction of having children, let's say a husband who, from his limited perspective, cares for her and is not physically or verbally abusive, and it earns her social respect in the eyes of her peers). Yet at its worst, the woman's whole life can become that of helpmeet, first, to her parents and then to her husband and children, to the point that she has no self-identity distinct from this role. She has no goals of her own, never explores her own abilities and talents independently of being a wife and a mother, never asks herself if she has the potential to make valuable contributions outside of the family, and makes no significant decisions outside of this role. Being generous spirited, even on occasion sacrificing one's own interests for those of others, are both morally unproblematic, but complete and permanent self-effacement such that one does not "exist" as an individual is deeply troubling. Historically it has taken a long time for the many formal and informal social constraints on even wealthy or middle-class women to be named and examined and for an increasing sense of dissatisfaction and loss to permeate the consciousness of women in these family settings. Many were and perhaps many still are quite content in this role. (I am referring only to women who adopt the goals and the life-path without question or scrutiny). The material benefits of coming from a well-off family and moving to a financially secure husband are major, and if we suppose the spouse to be generally kind and thoughtful in his limited fashion, then his wife may well be content. She is not suffering. She lacks the awareness of some critical aspects of her situation and is not discontent. Oppressive structures by no means always produce suffering, especially when we are speaking of civilized oppression (so set aside the formal constraints on the woman for the moment and focus just on the informal), and when, in addition, the victim has been thoroughly trained into the beliefs and attitudes that will make her a complaisant, even genuinely willing, party to her own oppression.

In Sam's case, I said that the actions may in a sense be right. A fair work environment, though, involves certain kinds of actions in the richer sense, actions where appropriate attitudes are involved in this "richer sense" of action. For example, challenging achievements will be recognized and the individual affirmed, but the book launch where Sam's book was "celebrated" really didn't include genuine celebration on the part of others in the department. Again, we can describe the acts in a primitive mode, referring to words spoken, smiles and nods, the raising of glasses, and so on, but in this situation none of this is genuine affirmation and the act of giving genuine affirmation did not in fact occur.

Only the illusion of it occurred and the fact that Sam may felt affirmed in no way establishes that he was. It was a sham. Yet in this example, the deception continues indefinitely for years, and that being so, Sam is not suffering in any clear sense.

My point here is that even so, the "fairness" of his workplace is illusory. Once we move to where Sam's professional life is actually lived, once we move to the departmental corridors, the offices where conversational exchanges take place or where review meetings are held, or to the classroom where the abusive student behaved so badly, then all of the components of Sam's professional life take on their proper significance. Issues to do with authenticity take on an importance that does not usually strike us when speaking at the more generalized level about the workings of some major institution where actual individuals, in all their full individuality, and their life-situations are not in the line of sight. For example, if we agree that the institution of social assistance is needed in a just society, we may then ask if the specific institution that has been set up is providing a fair amount and a fair distribution of money to those in need. Those at the distributing end of things have in mind thousands and thousands of recipients. Things like statistical analyses are likely to play a part in their consideration—if indeed any genuine consideration at all is given to the level of the assistance, if, that is, it is not all predecided by political fiat. Questions to do with authenticity, and in particular authentic moral relationships between specific individuals (e.g., the institution's representatives employed in the application offices), do not catch our attention in such contexts.

When thinking about more specific life-situations they do. In these situations we are far removed from realized major social institutions as such, and even further away from major institutions in the abstract, but we are where justice or injustice directly involves individuals. We are where people are respected or demeaned, where specific decisions are fair or unfair, where lives are enhanced or wrecked. Lives are lived in relationships and they are heavily involved in the immediate contexts of lived justice or injustice.

In Sam's case the decisions made are, in the bare bones sense, "correct," but the "collegial" relationships are deeply distorted. If someone slips up and the real nature of those relationships is revealed, he will be hurt, angry, and shocked. He will predictably feel a complete fool for being taken in by such deceptive appearances, even though he had no way of detecting the problem. He will feel deeply betrayed. He will suffer badly. Still, some things are even worse than such suffering, for example, if one can be spared the profound humiliation of such discoveries only by remaining, unknown to oneself, the subject of ongoing and concealed resentment, scorn, and denigration, by remaining a constant target for spite and malice, and by continually trusting where that trust is simply a vehicle for increased opportunities for thoughts and attitudes of contempt. The true nature of the relationships is completely concealed.

They are corrupt relationships that any self-respecting individual will wish to step back from so far as is possible, but not because the decisions made, the words said, the gestures and glances given—all construed in the primitive, behavioral mode—are not what they should be. In this thought experiment it is specified that they are. Had we the choice, we would step out of the relationships and remove ourselves as far as possible from them precisely because those basic actions do not reflect the beliefs and attitudes that should lie behind them, the attitudes that should be the source of those basic actions, and because the attitudes that *are* in place are demeaning, humiliating, and destructive to any reasonable sense of self-respect. The only thing worse than knowing how things really are here is not knowing.

Are these conceivable dangers a problem in the case of strangers? Sam, after all, has longstanding connections with others in the department. What if we are thinking of a customer at a service desk in a shop or what if the individuals have even less of an encounter than this? What is the relevance for complete strangers we never see, strangers perhaps on the other side of the world? Our thinking about these kinds of cases will depend on our positions on matters like the following: do we conceive of moral and political issues as distinct? Do we see the moral community, which permeates the whole of society (and not just the one we happen to be in) as carrying implications for social justice? Do we owe strangers anything? Do we have any moral obligations to those we have never seen and never will see? If we have some obligations with respect to the distribution of material goods to such complete strangers, why do we? Why and how do we see ourselves as in any way "connected" with them?

The commonly claimed role of major social institutions in a sound conception of social justice prompts us to think about the political and the moral sphere as independent, and it is clear at this point that I think this is short-sighted. It places false limits on the kinds of considerations relevant to a socially just society, to one that is not oppressive. I have been working toward a conception of the moral community, one that has practical moral implications for at least its agent-members. If fellow members include complete strangers we do not literally see and interact with, and if at least among fellow agent-members respect is owed (and I have argued for at least one form of respect, that embodied in inter-actional justice), then this "connection" does constitute a relationship, albeit of a kind unlike those we first think of. Such a sense of relationship is an ideal of a number of moral systems and religious theologies; it is a call to conceive of ourselves as in relationship with others not known to us and not seen by us. If we are connected even insofar as one kind of respect is owed to them, then it is conceivable to hold attitudes that con-flict with those called for by such respect. This is true even if we do not in fact ever actually "interact" with them. It remains a moral obligation to be, in principle, prepared to do so and to do so in good faith, that is, with the attitudes that are a component of that respect.

Although much work on justice via the distributive paradigm says little about relationships, the question remains as to why we should see ourselves as connected at all to strangers, whether in our own society or at a much greater distance. Why should "world poverty" be a pressing moral issue for us if the desperately poor are predominantly at a great geographical distance from us? There are of course very poor individu-als in every society, including the affluent Western nations, and not a small number of them, but it remains true that the number of destitute in some parts of the world is almost overwhelming—and they are far away from most of the Western nations. Should we intervene on the consequentialist grounds that it is safest to do so, that the very poor form a dangerously large population capable of wreaking havoc on our comfortable economic status quo? Should we do something because of the threat of "food wars," increased terrorism, massive illegal immigration, and so on? Is our obligation based on avoiding disastrous negative consequences of these kinds? Or should we intervene because doing so will bring the chance of a far better life for millions of people and will, it is thought, eventually enable them to move forward to further improved lives by relying more and more on their own resources? (This is quite a mixed bag of hope for consequences, including some that are self-focused on the part of the richer nations.) Or should we intervene because we should see ourselves as in community and moral solidarity as much with the very poor as with those around us, and if so, does this relationship of shared community bring with it urgent obligations to tackle the fact of widespread starvation, the thousands of deaths daily from illnesses easily preventable, the lack of basic education that condemns the people to a tragically limited set of future options and to a lack of leadership arising from within their own ranks? One thing I think is sure, that if we see shared community and the relationship it supports as foundational both morally and politically, then there emerge ways of thinking about others, not just acting toward others that involve morally suspect attitudes. I can act as I should and yet hold such attitudes, whether revealed or not.

In principle, morally distorted and derogatory attitudes need bring with them no specific consequences, yet I am arguing that they matter not only morally but politically. The sham of "fairness" in Sam's case illustrates how inner attitudes that are constitutive of the relationships that should hold in his work place can distort those relationships even when the attitudes are concealed and can change apparent justice into a mockery of the real thing. I am arguing, then, that there are non-consequentialist reasons for claiming that the mental lives of individuals, of a nation's citizens, play a key role politically, even when the beliefs and attitudes are not expressed overtly. Just as oppression involves the nature of the relationships, not simply overt and fairly "primitive" actions, so too does authentic social justice and we can see this most clearly at the level of a life lived, in the daily lives of individuals having to negotiate the actions of those around them, the interactions they engage in, the power structures they are faced with, and more. This is precisely the context of social justice that is most distant from that of the distributive paradigm with its focus on major social institutions.

The Irreducibly Individual in Authentic Social Justice

I contend that authentic social justice calls for certain attitudes to hold and to underlie "just action." I am not suggesting that it is appropriate for a government or any other institution to try to regulate or control minds, although I believe Tussman is quite right that there is not only a right but an obligation for a government to be thoughtfully responsible for public education. This should not involve the kind of attempted "control" that is so opposed to open inquiry. On the contrary, one primary goal of public education should be to promote the kind of exploratory skills and logical thinking that allow people to critique commonly held views, to think about alternative positions and fresh questions—in fact, precisely to equip people with a high degree of intellectual self-defense so that they are not subject to mental control by external powers, whether institutions or other individuals.

I claim that what happens in our minds contributes to social justice not only in the obvious consequentialist fashion (by prompting the actions that naturally follow from what is happening in the mind), but in a deeper, more intrinsic way, and that an exclusive focus on an over-simplified concept of action, one that relies on a primitive and heavily behavioral level of description, grounds a conception of "illusory social justice." It looks like the real thing, but it is not. Aspects of social justice that involve relationships are likely to involve the mental life of individuals in this way, and it is unclear at least that any aspect of social justice (including, as suggested above, fundamental issues to do with the distributive paradigm) is truly free from consideration of moral relationships. If so, what I call "authentic social justice" calls for a lot more from us than structuring the major social institutions wisely.

I am not advocating trying to regulate minds. It is in any case not feasible, but more importantly, it is not a morally sound way of aiming for those attitudes. They need to be morally endorsed: developed or adopted sincerely. Otherwise the lack of authenticity simply moves one stage back, to the minds of the members of the society. However, insofar as they connect with the possibility of authentic social justice, we are accountable for them and in these contexts a morally reasonable sense of privacy does not prohibit others from questioning us about our attitudes and engaging with us about them. In these contexts the familiar, inflated sense of rightful privacy about the workings of the mind is morally unsound.

Authentic social justice cannot be achieved solely by working on the major social institutions. As with interactional justice, it cannot even in principle be achieved by a top-down approach of that kind. Some elements of social justice are irreducibly from the ground up, from individuals as such. The attitudes and beliefs that transform often deceptive and primitively describable actions into authentic acts of fairness and justice must be contributed by the individual agents; they must be found in the minds of the individual players, and they are constitutive of authentic social justice. This conception of authentic social justice and the arguments in support of it again highlight the role of moral relations in thinking about social justice.

CHAPTER 7

A Rich Sense of "Responsive Reflection"

In this final chapter, I look back at some of the key points made about individual agent-victims of civilized oppression and consider their relevance to the nature of their agency. What moral agency can and should be exercised by the victims in particular? Some of the points argued for in earlier chapters are to do with the moral standing of the victims with respect to civilized oppression; some are to do with moral actions I have urged as their prima facie obligations; some are to do with the nature of certain relationships which, I believe, they either should enter into and develop, or should avoid or try to sever; and some are to do with mental attitudes that even victims, the most vulnerable and most hurt players in civilized oppression, should try to cultivate. That is to say, the agency referred to as morally desirable on the part of the victims covers far more than "actions" in the primitive, behavioral sense (a sense elucidated in the previous chapter).

Passive Victims

It is one of the main points in this book that victims of civilized oppression, although wronged, psychologically oppressed, and constrained by powerful others as well as by social institutions and structures writ large, should not be thought of as inevitably conforming to the stereotype of "passive victims," at least, not those victims who have a fair degree of agency-capability. To speak of victims is simply to speak of those at the receiving end of the power-backed oppression at work here; it refers to those who are systematically wronged and denigrated (whether overtly or otherwise) because of their membership in some despised group. Nothing more is built into the concept of victim as I use it. (In the remainder of this chapter I have in mind victims who have the capacities and abilities of moral agents.)

The victims do have special moral standing as victims, although it is not do with some kind of justified passivity. They have special standing in at least two respects. First, they have a claim on the community at large to the amendment of their situation, to compensation (if that is possible), to changes to the practices and structures that have left them victims, to the "repair" (to use Margaret Urban Walker's term) of the distorted relationships they have been maneuvered into.[1] And second, they have special standing in that they are an irreplaceable source of information, protest, and insights about civilized oppression.

The non-oppressed have an obligation to learn about oppression and in the case of this type, it is essential to learn about the powerful impact and moral significance of apparent trivialities inflicted on the socially disadvantaged. Since civilized oppression is inherently much harder to grasp than violent oppression (or oppression codified in law), the victims' experiences and accounts are even more vital than in cases of more blatant oppression. And since civilized oppression itself extends over a range of phenomena, which become increasingly subtle, there are whole ranges on this spectrum where input from the victims is not only valuable, but essential, if the nature of the oppression is to be grasped. We have already seen philosophers like Laurence Thomas, Elizabeth Spelman, and Christine Koggel emphasize the value of such input,[2] and Thomas bluntly asserts that if we lack such input, if the victims decide to remain "silent," then there is no realistic hope of understanding some types of social injustice.[3] Agent-victims have a prima facie obligation to inform the non-oppressed about the nature of the oppression, to convey, as best they can, some understanding of what is involved, to draw attention to the actions, including the less visible ones, that contribute to the oppression, and to explain the psychological oppression it produces. I have argued, though, that there are fully justified limits on this obligation, both for obvious reasons to do with their limited time and energy, and for less obvious reasons, such as the right to protect their self-identity from being manipulated into being solely that of "a victim of civilized oppression," a danger that paradoxically arises precisely when well-meaning others who are concerned to rectify the oppression consistently and frequently show moral deference to the victims.

I have spoken of educational initiatives on the part of the victims, but there are other initiatives also advocated in earlier chapters, for example, entering into relationships of moral solidarity with other victims of this and other forms of oppression (including with others—animals included—who are not agents but who are at the receiving end of oppressive practices), forming certain kinds of relationships with *some* agents who, all unaware, contribute to civilized oppression, responding with gratitude to, again, *some* contributing agents who break ranks with their privileged peers and pay an often unseen price for doing so. These are of course controversial proposals, but I have argued that some of them constitute non-standard forms of resistance to oppression, alongside the more usual kinds, like protest, appeals to observers, refusals to comply, and so on.

A fair number of philosophers argue that the oppressed have prima facie obligations that relate to their oppression, and not a few argue that victims have a prima facie obligation to "resist" their own oppression, although their grounds differ. For example, Laurence Thomas's call for the oppressed to speak up about their experiences, to take an active role in non-oppressed others coming to understand (hopefully, empathetically understand) what victims have to deal with is surely calling victims to at least one form of resistance. He points out that without such participation, the nature of oppression and its repercussions on its victims will not be understood. (This is especially so in the case of civilized oppression.) That is, the consequences of their failing to speak about their oppression are dire: the oppression will not even be grasped, let alone tackled. Bernard Boxill in his influential article, "Self-Respect and Protest," argues quite forcefully for the connection between protesting one's oppression and maintaining self-respect,[4] and in his later paper, "The Responsibility of the Oppressed to Resist Their Own Oppression," he is explicit that "it is [the responsibility of the victims] to resist, to show signs of power, and if they dare not show signs of power to their oppressors, to show signs of power to bystanders, or if even that is too hazardous, to at least resist in secret, in order to stave off the contempt of bystanders and their own self-contempt."[5] Carol Hay argues that the oppressed have an obligation to resist their oppression because they have an obligation to respect and protect the rational part of their nature, where this aspect of the self has value in its own right. Oppression, Hay claims, can harm our rational nature.[6]

The obligations are not open ended, given the limited time and energy victims have. And I have argued that they have no obligation of any kind to allow their self-identity to become solely that of "a victim of civilized oppression" (a matter of focus, rather than time and energy). Actions of victims that provide information and explanation of their oppressive experiences to the non-oppressed provide us with one of the most important consequentialist reasons for victim-resistance, especially in the case of the more subtle kinds of civilized oppression. On the other hand, Boxill's appeal to the connection between resistance and self-respect and the duty to oneself to protect self-respect (as best one can) presumably is one that he maintains even if the practical consequences are undesirable (e.g., an employment position is lost). And like other agent-members of the moral community, victims of civilized oppression are called upon to take the moral life seriously and exercise moral agency in various thoughtful ways. If they do not, the moral community will be a shadow of what it can and should be, just as much as if those who contribute to oppression hold back in the same ways. It will lack the strength, the energy, the warmth, and the hope it should embody.

Psychological Hurts and Relationships

What I wish to draw attention to here, though, is the very fact of this shared, robust call on victims to fulfill certain moral obligations. If I and a number of other philosophers are correct, then being a victim of civilized oppression becomes one aspect of one's self-identity and one that brings with it certain moral obligations. On this view, passive agent-victims of civilized oppression are actually failing in what should be their moral commitments. If we reject any stereotype about passive victims and call on victims of civilized oppression to fulfill certain obligations, we imply that they are in general not so psychologically wounded that they cannot exercise meaningful agency with respect to resisting their own oppression. The crucial claim I make about this is that this implication does not require a traditional conception of autonomy, an independent, autonomous self untouched by one's personal history and current social situation.

Throughout this book and in my earlier book, I have asserted that our lives are lived in relationships of various kinds, some more personal, some less so. As Christine Koggel points out, "We live our lives in relationships; relationships of support, care, nurturance, power, authority, powerlessness, oppression, equality, and inequality; relationships we value, take for granted, maintain, struggle in, and end."[7] Indeed, I conceive of relationships as holding with distant others who will never be personally known or even met by us (e.g., comembership in the moral community, or relationships of moral solidarity and/or some form of respect, whether mutual or asymmetrical). On my understanding of the notion of relationship, attitudes play a fundamental role and some attitudes can and should hold between complete strangers who never encounter each other in any way. (At least one form of respect of this kind is outlined in Chapter 5.) We do not live as isolated units but as embedded in networks of relationships. Furthermore, I have analyzed civilized oppression as, at its heart, to do with distorted relationships, to do with victims being placed in corrupt moral relations with powerful others. I say "placed" because the power differences at work are manipulative, systematic, and often intimidating and threatening (although not threatening of outright violence).

It is now a frequently made claim in feminist writings that living life in relationships is not only in practice inevitable, but all to the good. Not only are we all dependent on others in close relationships to us while we are infants and children, we exist in relationships of interdependency as adults and these relationships can be morally sound, satisfying, motivating in a good way, and sites of personal growth. By way of a stark contrast, Lorraine Code writes of a tradition where "autonomous man is—and should be—self-sufficient, independent, and self-reliant, a self-realizing individual who directs his efforts toward maximizing his personal gains."[8] Margaret Urban Walker's characterization is even more dismal. The individual is "disembodied, disembedded, unencumbered, affectless, isolated, detached, unpleasantly self-interested, defensively self-protective, abnormally self-reliant, and narcissistically self-reflective."[9] Whether or not this characterization is a fair representation of the ideal individual in traditional liberalism I will leave to others (e.g., see Will Kymlicka's denial),[10] but feminists in general reject any such "ideal," especially on the grounds that there is no acknowledgment of the relationships the person is in, let alone any favorable acknowledgment of relationships where the individual's empathetic caring and concern is central.

Clearly the condemned characterization of the ideal individual involves a lot more than that. Both Code and Walker specify the individual's overwhelming orientation toward personal benefit and gain, and Walker adds in the lack of any significant emotional life. These features are as repellent as the tacit denial of the role of relationships, and surely the inclusion of a number of negative features does make it much easier to reject the whole conception of such an "individualistic" person.

Being embedded in networks of relationships of various kinds and being oppressed means that in many of the relationships the oppressed are at the receiving end of relationship power. Within the realm of civilized oppression this means, among other things, being subject to socially constructed communication protocols that leave the major decisions about communicating to the socially privileged: they decide when to initiate a conversation, what the content and the boundaries of it will be, how long the exchange is to last for, when and how the interaction is to end, and so on. They have enormous interactive power (as I call it), all of it socially supported. The suggestion sometimes heard that the oppressed participant should "insist" on the nature of the content and on maintaining the conversation until what was meant to be said has been said, should insist on answers to important questions, should insist on an explanation of some threatening event or decision, should, in short, insist on being heard and responded to, is painfully naive. Of course it can all be attempted, but within the sphere of civilized oppression where no violence appears from any party, the oppressed participant cannot make the more powerful person stay longer if she decides to leave; she cannot make her give careful explanations or answer pertinent questions; she cannot make the biologically hearing person actually listen to what she is saying. With respect to the set of basic rights and obligations argued for in the earlier discussion of interactional justice, relationship power directed to daily life communication is, in itself, able to disempower victims of civilized oppression, both from having those rights fulfilled and from meeting the associated prima facie obligations. Being the victim of civilized oppression involves a lot more than this: being excluded, ignored, scorned, denigrated, subject to unfair and unpleasant characterizations, and so on. Violence is not required and neither is the use of law or institutional regulations. Such displays of relationship power are extremely easy to maintain without. The actual beliefs and attitudes underlying it all may not be voiced explicitly in the presence of the victims, and indeed the oppressors themselves may never have explicitly articulated them even to themselves. This, though, does not mean that the relationship power lacks impact.

Koggel refers to "the impact that relationships of all kinds have on self-concepts, identity, and self-determination,"[11] and I agree that the nature of the relationships we are in have a causal impact on our life-situation, on our opportunities, and on what we can actually do by way of life-affecting action. They can and do sometimes block actions outright, render them systematically futile, or turn them into a parody of the real thing. For example, relationships where the socially advantaged simply refuse to listen make a mockery of a victim's attempt to lodge a protest. She can say all the right words, but lodging a protest is not within her power; it is not a unilateral action. Similarly, being considered for an employment position involves a lot more than the applicant's sending in her resume. How it is received, the way in which it is read and thought about (if at all), is vital to the applicant's being considered for the position. Again, it is not an action she can perform unilaterally. Among other things, Koggel speaks of the impact of relationships on self-determination and when we think of actions that are potentially life-altering (like being considered for an employment position), it is surely true that the impact is often devastating, the more so since the distorted relationships lying behind that impact are not isolated and rare; they surround the victim. They entrap her in ways that result in systematic unfairness. The victims in their own right sometimes cannot—literally cannot—take any effective action against this impact, especially in the pressing time frame that so often actually holds. I have argued that there is a range of actions that can legitimately count as resisting civilized oppression (including educational initiatives and some things I have proposed that are more controversial). The actions are vulnerable to interference or nonrecognition, given who the would-be agents are, but presumably when ethicists like Thomas, Boxill, and Hay claim that the oppressed have an obligation to resist their own oppression, they are not requiring that they actually succeed.

We stop short of an adequate moral analysis, however, if we stop here. When we think of resistance, we need to say more about what we have in mind as the target site: are we thinking of their causal impact on the (overt) actions of the oppressed? or are we thinking of their effect on some other site?

Psychological Hurts and the Mind of the Victim

I mentioned above that calling on victims of civilized oppression to fulfill certain obligations means rejecting the claim that they are in general so psychologically wounded that they cannot exercise meaningful agency with respect to resisting their own oppression. But there is more than one site of the potential impact of oppressive relationships and actions, and it is important to distinguish them. The victims may not be able to respond effectively to them by acting in ways that change or undo them, so to speak, but when we consider carefully the idea of victims responding to oppressive phenomena, including powerful actions that cannot be undone, then we should also think about their intellectual response.

What role can the minds of the oppressed play? (I should say that this is not a critique of Koggel, but rather a line of thought prompted by her reference to self-determination.)

The fundamental point I want to make is that the mind is the site where passivity or resistance takes root; this is the overt action's ground of true rebellion. For example, even if the thought of resistance first arose because of discussion with others, if an agent's overt action is not afterward grounded in her own mind, it is not morally endorsed and not an expression of her own moral integrity. To say that victims sometimes cannot in their own right change the impact of certain pernicious, oppressive actions and are sometimes so constrained that they cannot perform acts of resistance in the usual sense simply does not tell us whether or not they are robustly "resisting" the injustice.

Ann Cudd claims that the intention to resist is a necessary condition in order to be said to be resisting oppression.[12] "Acts of resistance" of course typically refers to overt acts of some kind, and if we think of such paradigm cases, then it is not difficult to think of cases where the intention makes it impossible to describe them as resistance. Ferrying a small group of Danish Jews to Sweden because you are dared to do so and taunted as a coward if you do not does not make the action one of resisting the Nazis' oppression. One may even support the attempt to ship them to death camps but reluctantly set aside that support because one is angry at being called a coward. It is an action in the usual sense and one which, if successful, will save some Danish citizens who are Jews, but the motive is transparently wrong. Perhaps a more puzzling case is one where the nature of the wrong as systematic (i.e., as oppression) is not grasped by the one "resisting." For example, we can imagine someone's intervening to aid or rescue someone being wronged where this moral response is immediate and motivated by that very aim (to aid or rescue a victim of wrongdoing). Suppose also that he protests and condemns the wrong and that these moral responses of protest and intervention are ones the agent can be counted on to make in other situations of this kind. Yet he does not grasp that the wrong is of a kind that is systematic. The moral indignation toward the wrongdoing is there, the indignation and responsive moral actions are there, but the understanding that it is an instance of oppression is not. Certainly if more individual agents acted this way, oppressive acts would be somewhat lessened, but perhaps the underlying social structures would not. But in any case, the rescuer himself has not grasped correctly the moral nature of the situations (although he has clearly seen the wrongdoing). I suggest that if anything disqualifies it as a case of resisting oppression, it is this feature, not the expected lack of impact on the relevant social structures. In the main I am rather sympathetic to Cudd's claim that the intention to resist oppression is a necessary condition of its being resistance, at least in standard cases that involve actions of the usual kind, and her insistence on this can disqualify the description in the example given here.

Cudd goes on to say that

> A person or group resists only when they act in a way that could result in lessening oppression or sending a message of revolt or outrage to someone. My account does not categorize as resistance cases where the only ones witnessing the action are incapable of receiving a message of revolt and there is no lessening of oppression. Such cases are surely rare.[13]

Here I believe that Cudd greatly underestimates the significance of what happens in an agent's mind (intentions notwithstanding). I am all in favor of actions that "could lessen oppression or send a message of revolt" (which, if we stay within the sphere of civilized oppression here, will not involve violence). Even oppressed agents may sometimes be able to act in the full-blown sense (not in just a primitively behavioral sense, as I have spoken of it before this); for example, they are able to lodge a protest, not simply say the words that would constitute a protest if only they could get someone to actually listen to them. On the other hand, they may often be heavily constrained in their actions. It is not true, though, that someone so constrained is incapable of resistance. Agents can also take mental initiatives, some bigger, some smaller, and being heavily constrained in one's actions does not preclude a thoughtfully reflective response to the constraint.

Earlier in the chapter, I quote Bernard Boxill who writes that the victims of oppression have an obligation to resist their own oppression, and if it is too dangerous to do so openly, then they should "at least resist in secret," but he goes on to say "in order to stave off the contempt of bystanders and their own self-contempt."[14] It is clear that, according to Boxill, resistance must require *some* overt action, since he speaks of the response of bystanders to this "secret" resistance. His example is that of slaves who damage their tools, steal from their master, pretend to be stupid, turn up late, and in other ways frustrate the slave-labor agenda.[15] While agreeing with Boxill that resistance need not succeed in order to be resistance,[16] I am taking the range or site of such resistance one step further: if overt resistance is genuinely futile or highly dangerous or even in practice not possible, then there is still a form of resistance that remains, that of the mind. I am not suggesting that this site of resistance be kept in reserve, so to speak, for such situations. On the contrary, I think it should be thought of as a normal response of agents to significant life-situations generally, good, bad, and puzzling.

Imagine a Christian priest seized and subjected to solitary confinement for years (and I heard of such a case in my youth at a time when Christians were persecuted in the country I have in mind). He is aware that in this country and at this time, Christians, both lay and ordained, are oppressed. His actions are unbearably controlled. He cannot even interact with the jailers who bring his meager food ration. He cannot "talk to them" since they will not listen. He cannot even resist by declaring his faith to them; they listen to nothing and they are the only people he sees (or rather, he sees the hand that pushes the food tin through the slot and removes the slop bucket, and he sees their eyes watching him now and again). It may be that his faith position makes it inconsistent with his integrity to try to starve himself (whether or not that would qualify as resistance). In any case, I am claiming that even if, ex hypothesi, no physical action, either of commission or omission, that would count as resistance is feasible, we are still rushing to judgment if we declare he is not "resisting." His attitude of mind, his mental defiance, his determination not to be cowed into betraying beliefs that are so much a part of him, all constitute resistance to his oppressors and their goal of having him completely break down. And an attitude of mental defiance typically takes serious work. Wishing will not bring it about. There are thoughts and ideas to examine, fears to face, temptations to resist, times when it all becomes too much and one must shore up a much weakened sense of resolve if not indeed begin to build it up all over again. Action in the usual sense is certainly not the only site of resistance. There are, though, other types of actions, and developing a resistant mind will involve mental "actions"; it will not just happen.

Ideally, this would be developed with the support of those in various relationships with us and the support of the moral community. Marilyn Friedman refers to the "moral growth of a certain particular sort" that can arise out of a friendship: we learn our first values and moral rules in the moral socialization from early caretakers, but we are capable of "undergoing remarkable changes of commitment in later life. Friendship can be an invaluable source of such moral transformation."[17] The trust, intimacy, and disclosure that naturally occur within friendship allow us to think about moral standpoints very different from out own: "Through seeing what my friend counts as a harm done to her, for example, and seeing how she suffers from it and what she does in response, I can try on, as it were, her interpretive claim and its implications for moral practice."[18]

This is a beautiful example of how a relationship we are in can not only help us to reflect on our own moral and social situation, but can present fresh moral standpoints to explore. Our commitment to a friend is "to a person in her unique particularity,"[19] and the specific features of the relationship and the friend therefore provide a rich array of potential insights and leads.

I do find it strange, though, that Friedman insists that the relationship of friendship be "based on approximate equality (in at least some respects) and a mutuality of affection, interest, and benevolence."[20] In paradigm cases of friendship between two mature agents, the "equality" of personality, attitudes, emotions, and overall character and the mutuality of affection, interest, and benevolence are not unusual, but the importance given to it is very puzzling. Friedman writes that "Friends should be able to respect and take an interest in one another's perspectives. One friend's superiority in one area, for example, in breadth of life experience, need not give that friend a privileged place in that relationship if it is balanced by the other friend's superiority in some other area, for example, in vitality of imagination," the concern being that "Relationships that lack this sort of balance and mutuality would seem to reduce to something too hierarchical to constitute genuine friendships. They would seem, instead, to take on a master-apprentice or mentor-student quality."[21]

But friendship need not be mutual in all or even most respects (although the two qualities of mutual affection and trust, I think, are central). I have genuine friendships with my companion animals who display abundant affection for me and a huge amount of trust (both of which are reciprocated). "Benevolence" is a little different, at least construed as intentional acts of help. If explicit intentions are built into the concept, then perhaps animals are not benevolent. Much-loved companion animals clearly express trust and affection and, correspondingly signs of fear and distrust often signal past abuse and neglect. They do not have to be capable of intentional benevolence to be friends. And surely Eva Feder Kittay had a relationship of friendship with her much-loved daughter who was born with a severe mental disability,[22] yet intentional benevolence, I gather, was not something within her capacity.

Nor can I see the necessity for the kind of "balance" Friedman refers to where the "superiority" of one friend in one area is balanced by the other friend's "superiority" in another area. Interactions between friends involve a lot more than talking, although serious conversations undertaken in complete trust constitute one of the special gifts of many friendships. But I reject that they are essential to a friendship that is rich in value, and I certainly reject that there can be no moral growth, or even "moral transformation" arising out of that relationship unless we have the kind of balance Friedman refers to. The relationships between myself and my companion animal, and between Eva Feder Kittay and her daughter are in some respects noticeably asymmetrical (although not with respect to trust and affection). They are not relationships of "equality" in Friedman's sense. The differences in features between the parties in these relationships can privilege one of the parties, can in fact give power to that individual that can be immorally exercised over the other. This seems to be the legitimate concern of Friedman, but this does not make the relationship "hierarchical" in a pejorative sense. It does, however, make it *potentially* hierarchical in that morally tainted sense. The power difference is there to be misused—or not.

Such friendships can be rich, challenging, and morally sound, and I can learn from them. The sources of my moral growth are not restricted to those in relationships of equality (as Friedman uses it) or those who are "superior" (again, her term) in the respects affecting the relationship. For example, animals, young children, and those facing serious intellectual challenges may be untouched by corrupt social ideals: your dog loves you whether or not your clothes are the flashy ones you wore before you lost your job; the toddler picks out the pebble off the beach and carefully takes it home because it is beautiful, not because it is worth any money. Moral insights do not have to be complex to be profound. Yes, we can learn many things from these friendships.

However, it may not always be possible to develop mental resistance to civilized oppression by calling on the support of those in various relationships with us and the support of the moral community. Such resistance may not be visible to others, since it may not be feasible or even in practice possible for it to be accompanied by overt action. The situation need not involve violent oppression for the underlying point to hold: resistance of the mind is sometimes the only form of resistance possible and it is in any case a crucial component of endorsed resistance to oppression of an overt kind, and it is surely not "rare." Consequently I recognize an additional site of oppression to that recognized by Cudd.

When Koggel writes about the impact that relationships have on self-determination, I again wish to distinguish between the kind of self-determination we first think of, that of (overt) actions in the standard sense and what agents can do and develop mentally. One does not have to start with a clean slate, a pristine mind unaffected by one's previous personal history and current social situation, in order to take on the work of developing certain mental strengths, and the harder work of actively responding to our psychological hurts and slights (and they will be different for different people). Perhaps self-determination is too powerful a term, but "aiming to affect one's mind—a mind already affected by others and by our history, relationships, and social situation—by pro-active mental work" is, I claim, not too powerful a description.

Psychological Oppression

What are we to make of "psychological oppression" in all of this? Sandra Bartky writes that "The psychologically oppressed...come to exercise harsh dominion over their own self-esteem. Differently put, psychological oppression can be regarded as the 'internalization of intimations of inferiority,'"[23] which can have as its victims even those with material benefits.[24] Anita Superson notes that "under patriarchy, women are likely to develop desires that when satisfied support oppressive conditions and practices."[25] In civilized oppression these manipulated, "deformed desires" (as Superson aptly calls them) can function to make the victims self-complicitous in their oppression.

In the case of psychological oppression, we are ultimately talking about what is happening in the minds of the oppressed: their psychological state and hurts, their "emotional category configuration."[26] The key question here has to do with whether there is any essential passivity of victims of civilized oppression. What sense can be give to "aiming to affect one's mind—a mind already affected by others and by our history, relationships, and social situation—by pro-active mental work"? Nonpassivity involves activity of some kind, and what I call responsive reflection is nonpassive. There is a distinction between having been affected by the dominating and marginalizing practices of civilized oppression and our response to that fact, and I include here responses that involve no action in the usual sense.

Sandra Bartky emphasizes the impaired self-esteem that usually accompanies oppression. Responsive reflection does not require that one can wave a magic wand and fairly promptly restore one's self-esteem. It does not in fact require that we succeed in restoring self-esteem at all, at least in the sense of *feeling* confident of one's own "worth" (although that would obviously be desirable). If responsive reflection moves the victim forward to the realization that the lack of self-esteem is a result of the civilized oppression and is in fact a mechanism of subordination, then pro-active mental work is already in evidence. It takes more than a hunch or a suspicion to "realize" such an important fact; it takes reflective work and endorsement. It is a different kind of fact from knowing where the Eiffel Tower is: it constitutes a moral insight. It takes even more mental work, effort, and development to move to a further stage where the person, at least in some important situations, *acts* as though confident of his/her self-esteem while *feeling* very differently. That is to say, I think the traditional Kantian distinction is valuable here. (Again, feeling confident would be better.) None of this is to suggest that moving forward is easy, straightforward, or quick. It may take years of work, especially to develop a mind that can decide on some actions, at least in some situations, and successfully follow through, where those actions are in tension with the person's feelings. Also, none of this is to suggest that the work should be undertaken alone (except out of necessity), but in the final analysis it has to involve the individual personally and quite deeply; even the realization referred to above (as to why the person lacks self-esteem) cannot remain permanently a second-hand acquisition. We are thinking about victims with a fair degree of agency, with the mental capacities that this requires: to a fair degree they are able to think, explore, perceive, be aware, remember, predict, and so on. None of the above requires that we launch into a defense of some metaphysical "inner citadel" in order to refer to these capacities.

Exercising Our Judgment

In "Autonomy and the Social Self," Linda Barclay quotes from Will Kymlicka's *Contemporary Political Philosophy: An Introduction*:

> No particular task is set for us by society, no particular practice has authority that is beyond individual judgment and possible rejection. We can and should acquire our tasks through freely made personal judgments about the cultural structure, the matrix of understandings and alternatives passed down to us by previous generations, which offers us possibilities we can either affirm or reject. Nothing is "set for us"; nothing is authoritative before our judgment of its value.[27]

Barclay accuses him of being "guilty of excess" in his "enthusiastic claim"[28] and goes on go say that "If this is meant to be a claim about the psychological capacity of each and every individual, it disregards the force and pervasiveness of social determinism and is clearly false."[29]

Kymlicka is actually reporting what he sees as the traditional "liberal" view rather than speaking in the first person, and perhaps it is fair to say that the liberals Kymlicka is portraying are no doubt aware that some individuals with some of the features of moral agents are nonetheless so debilitated that they are severely restricted internally in their ability to exercise of the "judgment" referred to. Charitably construed, the claims are not about "each and every individual," but are surely meant to be claims about people in general.

Barclay rejects the claims, but I am puzzled by how "obvious" it is to Barclay that they are all "clearly false." The claim most open to indignant rejection is the first in the quotation, that "no particular task is set for us by society," which reappears a little later in the quote from Kymlicka when we read that "We can and should acquire our tasks through freely made personal judgments about the cultural structure, the matrix of understandings and alternatives passed down to us by previous genera- tions, which offers us possibilities we can either affirm or reject." One is reminded of John Stuart Mill's complaints about how the vast majority of people take up their life-path without "choice" since "he who does anything because it is the custom makes no choice."[30] They fail to exam- ine their deepest inclinations:

> In our times, from the highest class of society down to the lowest, everyone lives as under the eye of a hostile and dreaded censor- ship... They ask themselves, what is suitable to my position? what is usually done by persons of my station and pecuniary circumstances? or (worse still) what is usually done by persons of a station and cir- cumstances superior to mine?... It does not occur to them to have any inclination except for what is customary. Thus the mind itself is bowed to the yoke.[31]

The complaints are about people not acting on their examined inclina- tions in "choosing" their life-projects and pathways, and even though Mill explicitly mentions "classes of society" and "persons of my station," there is here a dismaying failure to see how the social structures externally control the actions of those without social power, how they can impose failure and futility on many such actions, if they can even be attempted. Both Mill (at least the bit referred to above) and the quoted liberal view are glibly unrealistic as written and in this I share in Barclay's rejection.

The quoted liberal stance, however, also contains a more interesting feature in its use of the term "authoritative," rather than "powerful," when it is claimed that "nothing is authoritative before our judgment of its value". Something being authoritative has to do with the standing or legitimacy, not the sheer power, of whatever it is. Some social practice or commonly held position or stereotype, for example, may have a powerful and unexamined hold on us, even if it is illegitimate and unworthy of such influence. The quote explicitly refers to the exercise of intellectual judgment, to the mental assessment of value, and I think it is here that Barclay and I differ. When she claims that what the liberal stance calls for is not within "the psychological capacity" of all (or most?) individuals, it is presumably this mental assessment of value.

This is a capacity I have said quite a lot about. It is perhaps worth noting that reflecting on what life brings is something that develops over time and it involves work. It is not like pressing a button and activating the capacity. Responsive reflection takes time and, to be fruitful, has to be continued (not obsessively) in the long term. As I have argued above, responsive reflection is consistent with having been impacted by one's personal history, the workings of oppressive social structures within it, and the relationships one is and has been in. The ability to develop such reflection is not automatically eliminated by nonviolent, social constraints on actions in the usual sense (which is the nature of the constraints on actions in the case of civilized oppression).

Responsive Reflection

There is more to a *rich* conception of reflection than responsive reflection to one's own oppressive experiences and situation. It involves drawing relevant distinctions, thinking back to other, similar cases and looking for their relevance, thinking about what this or that perception suggests about some action, some institution, vulnerable others, oneself, or those we love, assessing options that hover in the future, thinking back on decisions made, good and bad, wise and short-sighted, our own and those of others, and asking what can be learned from them, asking what we habitually do or do not do that we ought to try to change, thinking about what, morally speaking, are our strong points and what our weakest, calling upon our ingenuity to explore solutions to oppressive situations encountered, and so much more. There are things to be examined, puzzles to be explored, ideas to be assessed, and often there are others embedded in all of it. They may or may not be personally known to us. They may be fellow agents in the moral community, they may be non-agent members whose vulnerability or suffering speaks to us. But caring is not enough. Reflection involves skills, and like other skills, they develop only with commitment and over time. Even things as apparently simple as knowing what we habitually do are not simple in reality. Self-awareness and also the awareness of others and of our situations do not come easily or naturally.

Carol Hay argues that the oppressed have an obligation to resist their oppression since they have an obligation to protect their rational nature, a Kantian obligation toward oneself.[32] I sympathize with this move, since I believe that the rational, thinking, and exploratory capacities constitute *one* precious feature of agents in the moral community. None of this means that we have some kind of unambiguously inspired "starting point" for our reflection. Long before we have a chance of beginning seriously to develop a range of mature reflective abilities, we have lived quite a number of years, with all the encounters, relationships, hopes, disappointments, joys, betrayals, and so on that go to make up most people's lives. And since our focus is on victims of civilized oppression, they will have lived years in systematically distorted relationships with the oppressive phenomena that accompany them. We each have a personal history and in various ways it will have left its marks.

But there are some simple, albeit important, points to note. In the first place, a messy starting point does not automatically condemn us to staying on equally messy pathways. The victims carry with them memories of what civilized oppression involves: of hurts, embarrassment, shock, bewilderment, frustration, disappointment, and unpleasant discoveries, some of which have left some long-lasting effect. Yet this is where the commitment to reflection has to begin, in all the messiness of a life already much lived and in these cases, lived for much of the time in forms of social subordination. But there is indeed the potential for things to become clearer over time, for details that matter to be distinguished from details that do not, for main themes to emerge and be noticed, for these and other insights to be gained. Since reflection as I am thinking of it includes, among other things, a commitment to develop a number of skills, there is reason to believe that we can become better at it over time and can do so without its becoming the be-all and end-all of our daily lives.

A second simple but important fact is that there is a huge difference between, on the one hand, finding ourselves immobilized in oppressive ways that involve major injustice, and on the other hand, our passively accepting it. And here, by "accepting it," I do not mean declining to act against it when we could, but rather making no attempt to seriously reflect on it. There are cases where being blocked in oppressive ways is something we can literally do nothing about; no action on our part can make a dent in it because the kinds of actions that could are essentially non-unilateral, they require the participation or cooperation of some others who refuse to do what they should. None of this precludes our *intellectually, reflectively responding* to the situation, and if we do, then this part of our life narrative has not yet ended. We may not be able to physically change the situation at this point, but it is a moral right of the most basic kind to be able to think about it all, to examine it, to subject the whole sorry business to our moral scrutiny, even if necessarily in hindsight.

And moral scrutiny in these contexts is—or should be—a wide open exercise that begins by observing and noticing. At some point, connections suggest themselves, patterns of actions raise questions and concerns, the unexpected behavior of others calls for some kind of explanation, and so on. We do not in these kinds of exploratory responses begin with a neat set of already formed, specific moral principles covering a broad range of oppressive phenomena. Rather, we are trying to attend to and begin to understand the situations and we are, so to speak, calling upon ourselves for our honest responses, to see where they point.

Reflection is what makes an immobilized victim of civilized oppression (immobilized with respect to meaningful action) nonpassive. It is the doorway to the beginning of intellectual understanding and resistance. Ultimately, with more time and more work, or perhaps with the help of exchanges with others, we may begin to think of nonobvious, less immediate and direct action that may help bring change into an oppressive situation, action that itself takes time to initiate. Intellectual resistance can lead to further, more overt possibilities.

Intellectual Resistance

But how important morally is mental resistance itself? Consider two oppressed individuals. One is pressured by those around her and reluctantly drawn into some action of resistance. This resistance is initiated and sustained by the others; she joins in because she is pressured to do so. The second oppressed individual is trapped in a situation where ex hypothesi he can do nothing in the immediate context to exercise his basic rights: he cannot get the other person to actually listen to his concern or his objection and his reasons for it. The person he communicates with refuses to listen and simply leaves, moving into an office behind the security guard. (Build in as many conditions as you will to make this a situation where the victim is classically immobilized.) The second person, however, when left standing, immediately begins to go over in his mind what has happened. The more he thinks about it, the more sure he is of his entitlement to speak about his concern and the more outrageous the refusal to listen appears to him. We can even build into the case that the protest had to be heard right then and there for it not to be too late, for the other person not to retreat to his office, pick up the phone, and finalize the decision that he wished to protest. With respect to that decision, the would-be protester has been rendered not simply ineffective, but nonfunctioning. Nonetheless, I would suggest that of the two oppressed individuals, it is the second who resists his oppressive treatment rather than the first, even though the first takes part in an action of resistance. It is the second person who resists, who exercises his moral agency as one who fights against his own subordination, making full use of some fundamental weapons he has at his disposal: his own perceptual, exploratory, and thinking abilities.

Such reflection and exploration need not focus on one's own situation and experiences, although it would be strange if they did not prompt such responses. The life-situations or specific experiences of oppressed others can also trigger careful reflection. Also, there is nothing here that points to an individual who is inherently self-interested. In fact, thinking about one's own experiences does not mean thinking about one's own self-interest. Again, it would be odd if it did not include one's own well-being, given the pain of some oppressive treatment, but thinking about one's own situation and experiences includes thinking about others who share relationships with us and about what we see happening to others. And all of it can prompt other questions, concerns, and possible explanations that are no longer to do with either ourselves or anyone around us.

I mention above that being a victim of oppression does bring with it a special moral standing, notably as an irreplaceable source of information and understanding of what the oppression involves (especially with civilized oppression). It does not, though, bring with it any special standing with respect to moral judgment or moral character. In the case of violent oppression, Claudia Card argues that the moral character of its victims is threatened and too readily compromised by prudentially motivated acts of acquiescence or even cooperation with the oppressors.[33] In any case, victims of civilized oppression face the same struggles in a commitment to the moral life as do others. They can be expected to have insight into the nature of the victims' experiences, however, this is but a possible starting point for any moral questioning.

I have argued that a rich sense of responsive reflection to oppressive situations and experiences (both one's own and those of others) is central to the moral nonpassivity of oppressed victims. It is where genuine resistance to oppression is anchored. Engaging in, and developing the skills involved in, such reflection are obligations of all moral agents, including those who have been wronged. Hopefully agents have the opportunity to discuss their thoughts and questions with others, but not everyone lives in an environment of such free exchange. And even if we benefit greatly from engagement with others, the thinking work cannot be fully delegated for at least two reasons.

In the first place, given our focus on civilized oppression, many of the actions that form patterns of exclusion, denigration, and subordination are anything but highly visible. Socialized, habitual actions of subtle kinds are often involved. But only the victim herself can develop the skills of awareness necessary to perceive patterns of such actions and how they function. No one can do this for another; it is not like passing on a body of knowledge from one person to another. Even describing the apparently trivial actions does not ensure awareness of them, either in oneself or in others. Noting such patterns in the actions of oppressive agents takes time and the more subtle the actions, the longer it takes. And we should not underestimate how often all of us use subtle cues with effect. We raise an eyebrow, look away, decline to smile, give a barely perceptible nod, and dozens of other actions, and although these kinds of actions are at the extreme end of those involved in civilized oppression, they are extremely effective if they systematically target certain situations and those at the center of them.

Victims face the challenge of becoming increasingly aware of the actions of contributing agents, of the nonintervening bystanders, and even of themselves. This last matters since it is not unusual for victims of civilized oppression to develop habits, actions that, if noticed at all, appear innocuous and morally irrelevant, yet which smooth the way for the contributing agents. Someone accustomed to being turned away when trying to communicate with a socially powerful oppressor may acquire the habit of beginning conversations in an acutely tentative fashion, always first apologizing for interrupting and always asking if perhaps the person is "too busy" to talk right now. Such a habit is very helpful to the person approached if she wishes to dismiss the importunate victim. As always with such cases, neither the victim nor the oppressor need be aware of the pattern of action that has come to function here. Also victims should become aware of their own patterns of actions, since they themselves are quite capable of functioning oppressively toward members of some other group. Their being victims because of their membership in one group does not prevent their oppressing members of another group (or even a comember of the same group), particularly in nonviolent modes.

For anyone, then, whether a victim, bystander, or agent of civilized oppression, self-awareness of one's habits is necessary in order to begin to have control of these kinds of barely visible but highly effective actions, and this will take persistence and time. Even if someone else informs Emma that she tends to look always at the men around her when some organizational crisis suddenly arises, and even if she believes what she is told, this is really no more than an invitation to begin the work of developing more perceptual awareness of both her stereotype of men as ingenious problem solvers in a crisis (and by implication, her very different stereotype of women) and her habit of calling upon them when such ingenuity is needed. Only she herself can take on the commitment, since only a naive reading of the situation would restrict its significance to sudden and unforeseen organizational problems in the workplace. We can learn from the progress of society as a whole that it has been morally wrong to withhold the vote from women and that it has been morally wrong to penalize women in the workplace because they are the ones who experience the challenges of pregnancy, but only the person her/himself can become self-aware of longstanding and subtle habits and of the stereotypes and attitudes sometimes hovering behind them. So one essential component of the rich sense of reflection I have claimed is an obligation of moral agents is self-awareness. We have an obligation to work on this goal over time, not out of some narcissistic fascination with ourselves, but because we are greatly morally hampered if we do not. Self-examination and self-awareness are neither morbid nor a threat to self-respect. They are simply a natural and ongoing part of moving forward in our moral questioning and commitments.

The second reason why the thinking work of moral inquiry cannot be fully delegated is that we are working toward moral beliefs and positions, and a moral position or belief we hold is, by its very nature, one we endorse. I believe that the Eiffel Tower is in Paris, but I have never seen it and my reason for claiming it is all to do with second-hand information. For myself nothing much hangs on this belief and there is a sense in which I accept it but give no personal endorsement of it. Moral beliefs or judgments that I eventually come to hold are endorsed by myself even while being open to further review (e.g., if someone explains an oversight or error in my view). They stand in a different relationship to myself from beliefs like that about the whereabouts of the Eiffel Tower. Hard-won moral insights are not infallible nor even essentially final, but the thinking work lying behind them and the decision-like endorsement of them makes them in a sense personal; the commitments they bring with them become part of what my integrity consists of and so the underlying moral beliefs become part of my identity.

Some strands of this may remind us of the Kantian notion of self-legislation within morality and it is a notion I have considerable sympathy for, but the self who is working toward such self-legislation here is someone who has for years been subjected to oppressive social structures, institutions, and practices, and who therefore has experienced the impact of that subordination. All the particularity of one's own past and one's own experiences lie at the center of this situation. Have they left a mark? One would certainly expect so. Are we helpless to work toward aware-ness of such particularities, toward the beginnings of an understanding of the pernicious practices and how they function, toward the realization that so many agents of civilized oppression are, in many ways, benev-olent, well-meaning individuals with no intention to cause systematic harm and denigration, toward the ways in which we would, if we could, rewrite our personal narratives, and so on? This, I think, is not at all obvious and I believe it is generally false. Reflection in a rich sense and the growing awareness it gives rise to are the beginnings of moral insights in oppressive situations. Since the victims I am thinking of here have agent-potential, it is a primary obligation to do the best one can to take a commitment to the moral life seriously.

Why Victims Should Explore Their Self-Identity

Throughout this book, issues to do with individuals and civilized oppres-sion (and therefore, social justice) have formed a central theme. I have emphasized the role of relationships in the nature of civilized oppres-sion (and therefore, again, in social justice), and if relationships are cen-tral to such oppression, then we need to think carefully about the role of individuals in them. Thinking solely about major social institutions overlooks components of social justice that are especially pertinent to civilized oppression. Social structures and practices that denigrate, marginalize, and subordinate those belonging to certain groups ultimately involve individuals in their functioning, not only as their victims. To understand civilized oppression we need to understand the roles that individuals play (e.g., in nonviolent forms of interactional injustice and in social justice that lacks "authenticity"). Focusing solely on major social institutions cannot provide an understanding of the workings of civilized oppression. A socially just society (and so one free of oppression of different kinds), requires irreducibly individual contributions. In this book I have focused primarily on the role of individuals, relationships (including those at the societal level), and the moral community with respect to civilized oppression.

Christine Koggel refers to "the impact that relationships of all kinds have on self-concepts, identity, and self-determination,"[34] but it does not follow from this that the self-identities of victims of civilized oppression are simply determined by relationships, that the victims are bound to be passive in that respect, however involuntarily. (This is not a critique of Koggel.) Just as when reflecting on their moral situation (in the rich sense of reflection explained above) and the systems of power that constrain them, I believe there is some room for victims to move.

But why should victims of civilized oppression think seriously about their self-identity? Our self-conception may not be just inaccurate, but deeply flawed, especially prior to any ongoing reflection and work on it, and this matters for several reasons. First of all, if someone in a close and personal relationship to us is valued (and that includes, or should include, oneself), then it is one form of basic respect to try to get to know that "someone" better. Second, if our self-understanding is wildly off the mark, it is likely to color our responsive reflection on our situation and our moral exploration and assessment of it. Third, agent-victims, like other agent-members of the moral community, have an obligation to reflect on their moral character sometimes and to try to work on changes when appropriate. This too involves examining some aspects of one's self-identity. And finally, thinking about our self-identity in certain ways is a form of rebellion against the stereotyped identities imposed by civilized oppression.

Getting to know someone we value who is in a close and personal relationship with us is a natural expression of that valuing, at least if we approach it respectfully, not intrusively. I am not thinking of doing so because it will facilitate the interactions and make it easier for me to know what to do and what to say in order to keep the relationship running smoothly (although such consequences are likely). The motivation I have in mind here is not self-interest. Knowing someone better provides a richer basis for empathetic understanding, and other things being equal, such a relationship is appropriate with someone close to us. If that someone is myself, I think the same basic point holds: I have a prima facie obligation to try to empathetically understand myself as well as others, not (here) primarily because of expected good consequences (although there are some), but as an expression of respect.

Second, if my self-understanding is nowhere close to accurate, then I can expect it to be a major hindrance in my responsive reflection on my oppressed situation and what it factually and morally involves. For example, if I conceive of myself as very sensitive to unpleasant and unfair comments when in fact I am quite resilient to them, then predictably I will underestimate the severity and extent of verbal abuse in my oppressive situation (and probably of other victims analogously placed). If I conceive of myself as fair in my employment duties but am actually swayed by others I interact with if they display manipulative emotions, then predictably I will be vulnerable to making decisions that are unfair to others (especially others not present) but which increase my popularity with those expressing the strong emotions. I am then likely to seriously underestimate the demands that fairness make on me, which in turn is predictably going to leave me with an immature (but comfortable) understanding of fair procedures. My assessments of fairness in other contexts is highly likely to suffer in consequence. It is not reasonable, though, to expect agent-victims to take on an enormous amount of work on examining their self-conception before beginning to responsively reflect on their moral situation and life experiences and those of others and what these matters illuminate. But it is reasonable to work on both side by side, while being alert to the possibility that undiscovered things about their present identity may sometimes result in oversights or mistakes on their moral exploration of civilized oppression generally. And it is reasonable to expect that over the long term, thoughts and questions will become more apt, more focused, and more informed by their experiences of civilized oppression (although always be open to thoughtful review).

This brings us to the third reason for thinking about our self-identity. I believe the vast majority of victims of civilized oppression with agent capacity are able to exercise agency although usually in highly constrained circumstances. (As throughout the book, I make no analogous claims about cases of violent oppression.) It has been claimed in a number of places in this book that in spite of the systematic constraints, there is for agent-victims in general no necessary passivity that follows from their being victims. We have seen a fair number of philosophers (including myself) call upon such victims to take on certain moral obligations (like the obligation to be a source of information and insight about the oppression to the non-oppressed, to resist their own oppression in other ways, to form certain relationships in oppressive situations, to responsively reflect on the moral questions their oppressive situations and those of others raise, etc.).

Obligations to do with resisting civilized oppression as such, whether urged for consequentialist or nonconsequentialist reasons (or both) are not the only kind of obligations those with agency are called to take on. Like others with significant agency, there is an obligation to try to reflect on one's moral character. Being a victim of systematic wrongdoing does not bring with it any immunity to moral faults and failngs. And while recognizing the phenomenon of psychological oppression, I, like other writers who call upon the victims to fulfill certain obligations, do not accept that this can serve as grounds for stepping down from them, whether they are to do with civilized oppression and their role as victims, or to do with basic obligations of agent-members of the moral community.

As mentioned earlier, in the case of violent oppression, Claudia Card refers to "gray zones" where life-threatening dangers and extreme suffering lead victims to be complicitous with their violent oppressors for prudential reasons, often taking an active role in tormenting fellow-members of their targeted group.[35] Although there is a difference in how physically appalling the situations are, civilized oppression provides plenty of opportunities for analogous complicity. Those with agency have an obligation, now and again in a long-term fashion, to reflect on their moral character, ultimately in order to think about trying to make changes. But it has to begin with learning about oneself as one now is, and moral character is one important aspect of oneself. There is nothing new in this point; it has been made several times in this work, but it is one more reason why acquiring a more secure understanding of one's identity, of who one is, is an obligation, not an indulgence.

The final reason for thinking about our self-identity has a direct connection with what civilized oppression involves. Victims of civilized oppression are systematically subjected to exploitation, dismissal, scorn, and disrespect as members of subordinated and denigrated groups, and in many cases a victim belongs to more than one such group. Pernicious and contemptuous stereotypes are predictable. They grossly overgeneralize about the group-members and they infect the interactions between the stereotype's victims and society's privileged members. There are paradigmatic forms of these manipulations, where the negative conceptions, beliefs, and stereotypes of the oppressors are internalized; the victims are psychologically oppressed. The stereotypes generate strings of morally objectionable terms for which there is no analogous equivalent that applies to those with social prestige. And there are other, less recognized manipulations that emanate from supportive, non-oppressed others who "relentlessly" show moral deference to the victims (see Chapter 4). Interestingly both forms of identity-manipulation function to obscure or obliterate the individuality of the victim and I believe this is to be actively resisted.

Again, as discussed earlier in this chapter, the impact of the treatment (most importantly in the paradigmatic cases) is not denied, not on our life-situation and not on our self-conception, but this does not in itself dictate a passive nonresponse at the level of the mind. Given that the subject of reflection here is one's own self-identity and self-conception, the "collective" resistance to this deleterious component of civilized oppression necessarily involves a great deal of effort from individual victims. Increasing self-awareness about our self-identity is no more easily achieved than self-awareness about our own subtle habits, and making at least some headway on awareness of our present self-conception is needed before we can begin to reflect on it (in the rich sense of reflection emphasized in this chapter). Whether tackled alone or with the intended help of others, it is unrealistic to expect that a modest amount of time and effort will yield a detailed and correct set of answers. Nonetheless I think we have an obligation to take on the work and try to make progress (at least for the reasons given here), and since situations and relationships change and develop (for good or for bad) and since our own self-understandings and hopes can also be expected to change, the commitment is very much a long term one.

As annoying as the aforementioned quotation from Mill is in its disregard for oppressive constraints on the actions of some in society (e.g., what he refers to as the "lower classes"), he is right that self-identity thrives when translated into actions and into our relationships—when we live out who we are. However, his portrayal of how simple it is to locate our self-identity and then to express it in a rich range of actions and projects (and relationships) is highly misleading and selective. Locating elements of one's current self-conception is an enormously challenging task. Moving to "making changes" by taking on new actions or modifying those we now perform is something further.

What if victims of civilized oppression are so constrained by the power-backed actions of others that they cannot in practice even try for the life-path they have come to desire? I gave my answer in Chapter 4 in connection with a nonstandard constraint on an oppressed's self-identity. Briefly, dreaming about what one would do if able to secure the fair cooperation of others, even when in fact it cannot be done, is not a kind of indulgence. It is not wasted time and mental effort that should be given to more direct forms of resistance to the oppression. Resisting any stereotyped identity not of our choosing is a form of resisting oppression. If actions are heavily controlled externally, then "staking a claim to individuality, even if mainly via the resources of the mind, *is* fighting for the cause." I believe it is as important to explore one's individuality as it is to be in solidarity with one's fellow oppressed. It is an unusual kind of resistance, though, since unlike some other forms (such as protest, public refusals to comply, or taking educational initiatives), it resists the civilized oppression precisely by turning away from it.

The Default Position

To reflect on one's self-identity is neither narcissistic nor selfish, nor a denial of relationships and their importance. Always when beginning to reflect seriously on something, we have to begin where we are, and for victims of civilized oppression, this means with a self-identity already affected by years of subordinating treatment, with confusions they have been socialized to leave unquestioned, and self-denigrating beliefs and stereotypes that may have already been adopted. In trying to understand oneself as one now is, Robin Dillon captures the typical start position beautifully when she writes:

> I think of myself in certain ways, and at some level I know my self-image is not accurate. It incorporates distortions and stereotypes, half-truths and whole falsehoods; but it is handy, and it provides a lot of excuses for what I do and why I cannot change, at least not now. But insofar as I "know myself" in this way, I am not respecting my reality. I am not taking seriously the complexity of my self, the ways in which this image may be close to the truth and the way in which it is far off the mark.[36]

Dillon is aware that certainly if I *begin* to think seriously about myself in an attempt to come to "know myself," I am going to start in the usual default position of having hunches, wishful thinking, but also manipulated feelings of inadequacy or guilt that are uncritically turned into indicators of the associated failings and faults. It is just as likely that actual failings and faults receive no special attention from me if they are not generally socially condemned, or if they are not condemned in members of my group. For example, if someone is socialized into being servile to those in publicly assigned positions of "authority," then this may be welcomed by those with prestige and yet be a moral fault that leaves me silent when I should be speaking on behalf of some very vulnerable and mistreated others. It is also a failure of self-respect (and perhaps more controversially, a failure to respect the agency of those I am servile to).

Another problem in understanding myself as I now am is that many features of character and personality are articulated via what are called "spectrum concepts." To clarify briefly, the light spectrum contains all the colors of the rainbow. One stripe is definitely red and one is clearly orange, but there is no sharp line dividing them. There is a small zone where it is neither clearly red nor clearly orange. Spectrum concepts share this feature. There are clear cases where the concept applies and clear cases where it does not, but there is also a small area where no definitive answer can be given, not because of any inadequacy on the part of the concept user, but because of the very nature of the concept.

We have all seen people who are appropriately confident about their skills or talents, and we have all seen individuals who are blatantly arrogant, but when do we see signals that someone is sliding from the first attribute to the second? It matters for our self-understanding that so many personal attributes that are generally desirable have a shady "relative" lurking in the background. Reasonable confidence can move into arrogance, sensible caution into immobilizing fear, independent thinking into a wilful refusal to listen. Am I someone who works well in a team or someone who is all but dependent on others and cannot function well alone? Am I an impressive multitasker or someone who cannot prioritize and let some things go? When do we have a person who can give clear and unambiguous directions to others and secure their responses, and when do we have someone who shows signals of being a power-driven bully when in a position to be so? In all of these, there are crystal clear exemplars of each of the pair, cases where there is no doubt as to the answer to the question. However, there are also situations where there is no straightforward way to give an answer and this is frustrating when in the process of trying to know oneself (or others).

And knowing myself as I now am involves a great deal more than working to perceive aspects of myself that have a fairly direct moral bearing on my actions, attitudes, and interactions. Anyone undertaking this work on behalf of onself will be an agent-member of the moral community, given the capacities the undertaking involves, but there is much about any one person that has no obvious moral relevance. The memories that are cherished, the kinds of books read for enjoyment, the scenery we feel most at home in, what it is about this friend we most treasure, the quirky things we do that really have no point to them, and hundreds of other things are part of who we are, alongside our moral insights, blunders, oversights, the relationships we commit to and those that are imposed upon us, and so much more. Each person, and in fact very many nonpersons (consider our companion animals), are complex, unique, and fascinating if we move past the outer perimeter of the publicly visible self. In writing about self-respect, Robin Dillon points out that traditionally the self deemed worthy of being respected is a "generalized self," such as one who has "the capacity for rational autonomous agency."[37] She rightly and insightfully points out that generic descriptions of this kind cannot capture "me," a unique individual with attributes and aspects that extend far beyond any such attribute. Ironically the traditional conception of the self that is to be respected "involves self-erasure."[38]

Dillon's project is to do with a feminist conception of self-respect, but a number of her key points apply to thinking about self-identity as such. Agent-members of the moral community have their own personal features and peculiarities, interests and aptitudes; they are situated within various relationships, some chosen, some not, and subject to the prevailing social practices that, in the case of victims of civilized oppression, impose hardship and constraints, the details of which take on a specificity and uniqueness that is a natural consequence of the unique details of the individual's position. Dillon here reminds us of the complexity of the task, given the complexity of the situated self in any one case. The work involved is the same as that discussed earlier in the chapter: the full range of responsive reflection, now turned to questions of self-identity. It will therefore be difficult, slow, and need a long-term and ongoing commitment. Developing perceptual acuity and patience is essential for work of this kind; one cannot understand what has not been focused on, on what (here) has not been seen. And although mistakes and oversights are highly likely, and although there may be no point at which the person may be confident of having got it all right, this is quite consistent with an expectation of genuine progress.

Dillon seems to advocate much the same work on observing and learning about my present self-identity as I do. In thinking about self-respect, Dillon points to the dangers of not seriously examining who I now am. If I do not tackle the work, then

> I avoid confronting the aspect of myself that I experience as fragmented or contradictory, refuse to acknowledge the ways in which I am alienated from aspect of myself, ignore the fact that there is much about myself that I disown or suppress. But respecting myself involves acknowledging these aspects of myself and my relation to them, regarding them as warranting my attention, and dealing with them: working to integrate, transform, or get rid of them, or learning to live in acknowledged tension with them. The kind of self-understanding that such activities involve lies, I believe, at the very heart of self-respect.[39]

With this I agree. I claimed earlier that if we value and respect someone in a close and personal relationship with us, then it is an expression of that valuing to try to come to know the other better. And although Dillon does not use the phrase "moral character" here, I think it is clear that she is sympathetic to the idea of examining that component of oneself. One of several possible reasons for "disowning or suppressing" some elements of myself is the growing realization that I cannot morally support those elements. But setting long-term goals to make some changes to one's moral character is not an option if there is no self-awareness of it as it now is, with both its weaknesses and strengths. Also I have argued that increasingly accurate self-knowledge is vital if we are to understand and come to resist an oppressively determined self-identity, and equally so if misconceptions about oneself are not to interfere with responsively reflecting on an oppressed situation and what it factually and morally involves. Hopefully the patient work of coming to understand oneself can move forward with the help of others, especially those we trust who are in special relationships with us, but move forward it should. All the reasons why (given above) are moral in kind; they involve explicit or implied obligations (some of which are to oneself). In short, as stated so often in this book, for those with agent potential (which I believe includes most of the victims of civilized oppression), being a victim does not justify a morally passive way of being, nor does it excuse someone from the basic obligations of agent-membership in the moral community.

This chapter has been about matters to do with victims of civilized oppression with agency, since to undertake the full range of responsive reflection referred to one has to have the capacities agency requires. The moral community I envision includes more than these, and more than all those with agency. Obligations and responsibilities fall to the lot of agent-members, but interactions and relationships of rich and various kinds are not so restricted. Relationships do not have to be between agents (or even involve an agent at all), nor do they have to be intentionally initiated in order to be precious and a source of joy for those in them and sometimes those who observe them. (And who has not on occasion had glimpses of a relationship where you are not personally involved, where the parties to it are strangers to you, and yet where you walk away smiling?)

The Moral Life and Cynicism

Among other things, the work in this book takes moral agency seriously (even under conditions of civilized oppression), the moral community, moral relations between members of the community (sometimes very differently placed in society), the life of the mind, the value of personal relationships, and the capacity of those with agency to care for and about the vulnerable, acquire highly developed perceptual skills, take on life-affecting reflection and moral exploration, give a fair amount of effort to serious concerns that do not affect them personally, and have the generosity of spirit to genuinely celebrate others and their achievements. It does not need to be said that I am not a psychological egoist.

Students en masse these days blandly assert that everyone acts always from the motive of self-interest (and this before even hearing of Hobbes!). Some academic disciplines actually start with that unexamined assumption as a premise. I have always found this both odd and disturbingly self-justifying: if the claim is true, I have no need to explain why I did what I did, since it is what everyone does all the time. And presumably it would be unreasonable to expect anything different from me since it is just "human nature." It is a thoroughly unconvincing position since, when all is said and done, the claim that everyone always acts from this motive is empirical. We can allow that some people may be self-deceived about their motive, but the underlying claim that the *real* motive is always self-interest remains solidly factual. That being so, it is at least conceivable (whether or not in practice possible) that things could have been otherwise. With a genuinely factual claim, we should be able to conceive of its being false. We should, then, be able to articulate what someone's acting on a motive other than self-interest would look like. Then I can, so to speak, go out and look for the relevant evidence, one way or another. If I cannot even articulate what a counterexample would look like, then I cannot look for both favorable and unfavorable evidence and see what I find. I have yet to hear a student who makes this sweeping claim about motives go on to articulate what a counterexample would be like *if* we were to find it. What happens, as all instructors know, is that they insist on the claim's being true, rather than test it, and so for any case presented to them, ingeniously think of a way it could be motivated by self-interest. I have never doubted the ingenuity of most students, but of course, this process has nothing to do with patiently checking out the truth of a empirical general claim. The question is what the motive actually was, not what someone can ingeniously imagine it to be.

And the same point holds for claims about self-deception: we need to be able to test for the truth of any claim that in this or that case, the agent is deceived about his motive. There are sometimes reasonable grounds for such a claim, if, for example, a pattern of actions is in conflict with the avowed motive. That this can occur is not the problem. There is of course a problem if in every case where an agent claims the motive was altruistic, there is the same kind of insistence that this claim is false, that self-deception must be involved. Is it *conceivable* that every such claim be false? Of course. But what are the criteria that distinguish a true claim about one's motives from a self-deceived claim? (The expectation that the agent's *actions* are in line with her claimed motive will certainly not be sufficient to provide grounds for the sweeping claim of psychological egoism.) What would a true claim about the motive being altruistic look like? Whether or not we ever find such a case, we should be able to articulate what it would be like and how we would recognize it. And in passing, it is interesting and very revealing that in over 40 years of students giving "examples" of agents claiming one motive when in fact they are self-deceived about it, every example has been in the same direction: that of an agent sincerely claiming an altruistic motive when "in fact," it was self-interested. I have never heard anyone offer even a *conceivable example* of an agent sincerely claiming to have acted in his own interest when in fact he acted altruistically. The underlying bias is continually at work.

I think one has to be ideologically committed to the view that people are incapable of altruism to take it seriously, given the kinds of tortuous redescriptions of actions and attitudes it relentlessly requires. People sometimes do small, ordinary acts against their self-interest in their daily lives and sometimes do extraordinary things for people they do not know and may never even meet. We can also be selfish, oblivious, dismissive, and unfair, but even here, I see no reason to deny that individuals can and do sometimes change over time and that communities as a whole sometimes come to embody changes for the better at the level of prevailing social practices or major social institutions.

I find an ally in Trudy Govier, who writes,

> The attitude of mocking cynicism is one of generalized distrust in human nature and behaviour...No matter what might seem to be the case, things are bound to be rotten underneath. The mocking cynic laughs bitterly at the very idea that people might be altruistic, idealistic, or even just plain conscientious. Cynical laughter is...a bitter amusement at the very idea that people could be good and institutions properly conducted. Such notions merit only ridicule.[40]

She goes on to make an analogous point to that made above:

> The spurious universality of cynicism is just what proves it to be incorrect. Because the mocking cynic can impose his interpretation on any action or event, his superficially persuasive interpretation shows nothing illuminating about any particular event...Cynics may think they have exposed our deepest motivations, but they merely impose a model on actions and events.[41]

Whether we "insist" on the truth of a general empirical claim or "impose" a fixed interpretation or model on every action and event encountered, what we are doing does not qualify as anything close to acquiring knowledge. Dragging in the phrase "human nature" does nothing to raise the epistemological credentials of the general claim insisted upon. It is false in its own right (with abundant evidence to that effect), but unfortunately has the capacity to become self-fulfilling in sinister ways if uncritically and widely accepted. As Govier concludes, "Mocking cynicism is a trap—logically, personally, ethically, and politically. We should escape from this trap with trust and hope."[42] If agent-victims of civilized oppression are to play their part in resisting and, in the longer term, radically reducing this oppression, the trap of falling into cynicism has to be avoided, just as does a misconception of oneself as a necessarily passive recipient—both physically and mentally—of disparaging treatment and injustice. Given the nature of civilized oppression and the irreducibly individual components in it, embracing agent-membership in the moral community and the rich moral life associated with it are forms of political action. The challenges, disappointments, and uncertainties, the shining moments and the bleak times, the various relationships entered into or imposed upon us, all these and more go to make up the tapestry of civilized oppression, resistance, and political change. The work is there to be done. The adventure is there to be lived.

Notes

1 Introduction: Further Discussions of Civilized Oppression

1. Claudia Card, *The Atrocity Paradigm* (New York: Oxford University Press, 2002).
2. Ibid., 9.
3. Jean Harvey, *Civilized Oppression* (Lanham, Maryland: Rowman & Littlefield, 1999).
4. Harvey, *Civilized Oppression*, 86–89.
5. Elizabeth V. Spelman, *Inessential Woman: Problems of Exclusion in Feminist Thought* (Boston: Beacon Press, 1988), 178.
6. Laurence Thomas, "Moral Deference," *Philosophical Forum* 24, no. 1–3 (1992), 247.
7. Ann E. Cudd, *Analyzing Oppression* (New York: Oxford University Press, 2006), 195.
8. Laurence Thomas, "Moral Flourishing in an Unjust World," *Journal of Moral Education* 22, no. 2 (1993). 83–96.
9. See, for example, Sandra Bartky, "On Psychological Oppression," in *Femininity and Dominion: Studies in the Phenomenology of Oppression* (New York: Routledge, 1990), 22–32.
10. For example, Brian Barry speaks of being "concerned with justice in its wholesale rather than its retail form—with institutions rather than individual outcomes," which is an attractive but misleading metaphor for a top-down conception of social justice: Brian Barry, *Theories of Justice* (Berkeley: University of California Press, 1989), 354–355.
11. Joseph Tussman, *Government and the Mind* (New York: Oxford University Press, 1977).

2 Civilized Oppression and Gratitude

1. Daniel Lyons, "The Odd Debt of Gratitude," *Analysis* 29, no. 3 (January 1969), 92–97.
2. Ibid., 92.
3. Ibid., 93. Perhaps Lyons sees returning the wallet as such a paradigmatic instance of obligated help that he sees it as an obligation even if forms of benevolence constitute an imperfect duty, something that for my purposes, I need not address here. This seems more plausible than thinking that Lyons sees it as tightly connected with a perfect duty not to steal, since just leaving the wallet on the ground does not constitute stealing it. But again, it is not the focus of the main points.
4. For example, Fred R. Berger, "Gratitude," *Ethics* 85, no. 4 (July 1975): 299–301; A. D. Walker, "Gratefulness and Gratitude," *Proceedings of the Aristotelian Society* 81 (1981): 48; Roslyn Weiss, "The Moral and Social Dimensions of Gratitude," *Southern Journal of Philosophy* 23, no. 4 (1985): 495.
5. For example, Keith Dowling, "Expressing Gratitude and Feeling Grateful," South African Journal of Philosophy 15, no. 1 (1996): 23–28, Berger 299, and Weiss, 495.
6. For example, Dowling; Berger, 299; Weiss, 495.
7. See, for example, John Hospers, *Libertarianism* (Los Angeles: Nash Publishing, 1971); Tibor R. Machan, *Individuals and Their Rights* (La Salle, IL: Open Court, 1988); Jan Narveson, *The Libertarian Idea* (Philadelphia: Temple University Press, 1988); Robert Nozick, *Anarchy, State, and Utopia* (New York: Basic Books, 1974).
8. See, for example, G. A. Cohen, *If You're an Egalitarian, How come You're so Rich?* (Cambridge, MA: Harvard University Press, 2000); Virginia Held, *Feminist Morality: Transforming Culture, Society, and Politics* (Chicago: University of Chicago Press, 1993); Nancy Hirschmann, *Rethinking Obligation* (Ithaca, NY: Cornell University Press, 1992); Kai Nielsen, *Equality and Liberty* (Totowa, NJ: Rowman & Allanheld, 1985).
9. Peter Singer, "Famine, Affluence, and Morality," *Philosophy and Public Affairs* 1, no. 3 (Spring 1972): 229–243, and "Rich and Poor," in his *Practical Ethics* (Cambridge: Cambridge University Press, 1979), 158–181.
10. Lyons, 96.
11. Margaret Urban Walker, *Moral Understandings* (New York: Routledge, 1998), 131.

12. Elizabeth H. Wolgast, *The Grammar of Justice* (Ithaca, NY: Cornell University Press, 1987), 5.
13. Wolgast, 11–12.
14. Iris Marion Young, *Justice and the Politics of Difference* (Princeton: Princeton University Press, 1990), 27.
15. See, for example, Thomas E. Wartenberg, *The Forms of Power* (Philadelphia: Temple University Press, 1990), and J. Harvey, *Civilized Oppression* (Lanham, MA: Rowman & Littlefield, 1999), especially chapter 3.
16. Berger, 302.
17. Ibid., 301.
18. Claudia Card, "Gratitude and Obligation," *American Philosophical Quarterly* 25, no. 2 (April 1988): 115–127, 124.
19. Ibid.
20. Ibid.
21. Ibid.
22. Ibid., 117.
23. Harvey.
24. Card, 117.
25. Immanuel Kant, *Lectures on Ethics*, trans. Louis Infield (Indianapolis, IN: Hackett, 1963), 118.
26. Ibid., 118–119.

3   The Relationship of Moral Solidarity

1. Jean Harvey, *Civilized Oppression*, (Lanham, MD: Rowman and Littlefield, 1999), 70–72.
2. A number of writers have made this point, for example, Laurence Thomas, "Moral Flourishing in an Unjust World," *Journal of Moral Education* 22, no. 2 (1993), 87.
3. Ibid., 86.
4. Elizabeth V. Spelman, *Inessential Woman: Problems of Exclusion in Feminist Thought* (Boston: Beacon Press, 1988), 179.
5. Ibid., 179–180.
6. Ibid., 178.
7. Laurence Thomas, "Moral Deference," *Philosophical Forum* 24, no. 1–3 (Fall–Spring 1992), 247.
8. Thomas, "Flourishing", 91.
9. Ibid., 85.
10. Ibid., 86.
11. Thomas, "Deference," 246.

12. Ibid., 247.
13. Sandra Lee Bartky, "Sympathy and Solidarity," in *Sympathy and Solidarity and Other Essays* (Lanham, MD: Rowman & Littlefield, 2002), 71–72.
14. See Harvey, 86–92, on well-intentioned motives for "blaming the victim," where the latter is used as morally pejorative term.
15. Michele M. Moody-Adams, "Culture, Responsibility, and Affected Ignorance," *Ethics* 104, no. 2 (January 1994), 291–309.
16. Ibid., 301.
17. Paul Benson, "Blame, Oppression, and Diminished Moral Competence," in *Moral Psychology: Feminist Ethics and Social Theory*, ed. Peggy DesAutels and Margaret Urban Walker (Lanham, MD: Rowman & Littlefield, 2004, 183–200.
18. Ibid., 185–186.
19. Ibid., 188.
20. Ibid.
21. Bartky, 72.
22. Ibid., 72–73.

4 Moral Community, Solidarity, and Civilized Oppression

1. Eva Feder Kittay, "At the Margins of Moral Personhood," *Ethics* 116 (October 2005): 122.
2. Laurence Thomas, "Moral Flourishing in an Unjust World," *Journal of Moral Education* 22, no. 2 (1993), 93.
3. See Jean Harvey, "Reversing the Charges," in *Civilized Oppression* (Lanham, MD: Rowman and Littlefield, 1999), 79–100.
4. Ann E. Cudd, *Analyzing Oppression* (New York: Oxford University Press, 2006), 195.
5. For example, see Iris Marion Young's chapter on "Five Faces of Oppression," in her book, *Justice and the Politics of Difference* (Princeton: Princeton University Press, 1990).
6. Cudd, 192–193.
7. Lisa Heldke and Peg O'Connor, ed., *Oppression, Privilege, and Resistance* (New York: McGraw Hill, 2004), 561.
8. Ibid., 179–180.
9. Elizabeth Spelman, *Inessential Woman: Problems of Exclusion in Feminist Thought* (Boston: Beacon Press, 1988), 178; and Laurence Thomas, "Moral Deference," *Philosophical Forum* 24, no. 1–3 (Fall–Spring 1992), 247.

10. Thomas, "Deference," 247.
11. Thomas, "Moral Flourishing," 93.
12. Ibid., 87.
13. Ibid., 94.
14. Thomas, "Deference," 240.
15. Cudd, 198.
16. Sandra Bartky, *Femininity and Domination: Studies in the Phenomenology of Oppression* (New York: Routledge, 1990), 24.
17. Hilde Lindemann Nelson, *Damaged Identities, Narrative Repair* (Ithaca, NY: Cornell University Press, 2001), 21.
18. Ibid.
19. Bartky, "On Psychological Oppression," in *Femininity and Domination*, 22.
20. Marilyn Frye, *The Politics of Reality* (Freedom, CA: Crossing Press, 1983), 4.
21. See, for example, Bernard R. Boxill, "Self-Respect and Protest," *Philosophy and Public Affairs* 6, no. 1 (Fall 1976), 58–69; Robin S. Dillon, "Self-Respect: Moral, Emotional, Political," *Ethics* 107 no. 2 (January 1997), 226–249, "How to Lose Your Self-Respect," *American Philosophical Quarterly* 29, no. 2 (April 1992), 125–139, "Toward a Feminist Conception of Self-Respect," *Hypatia* 7 no. 1 (Winter 1992), 52–69; Marilyn A. Friedman, "Moral Integrity and the Deferential Wife," *Philosophical Studies* 47 (January 1985), 141–150; Thomas E. Hill, "Servility and Self-Respect," *Monist* 57 (January 1973), 87–104; Thomas E. Hill, "Self-Respect Reconsidered," from his *Autonomy and Self-Respect* (Cambridge: Cambridge University Press, 1991), 19–24; Diana T. Meyers, "The Politics of Self-Respect: A Feminist Perspective," *Hypatia* 1 no. 1 (Spring 1986), 83–100; Michele M. Moody-Adams, "Race, Class, and the Social Construction of Self-Respect," *Philosophical Forum* 24 (1992–1993), 251–266; Laurence Thomas, "Self-Respect: Theory and Practice," in *Philosophy Born of Struggle*, ed. Leonard Harris (Dubuque, IA: Kendall/Hunt, 1983), 174–187; Laurence Thomas, "Rawlsian Self-Respect and the Black Consciousness Movement," *Philosophical Forum* 9 (Winter-Spring 1978), 303–314.
22. Cudd, 195.
23. Cheshire Calhoun, "Responsibility and Reproach," *Ethics* 99 no. 2 (1989), 389–406.
24. Ibid., 401.
25. Ibid.
26. Ibid., 404.
27. Ibid., 405.

5 The Irreducibly Individual: "Interactional Justice"

1. See, for example, G. A. Cohen, "Where the Action Is: On the Site of Distributive Justice," *Philosophy and Public Affairs*, 26 (1997), 3–30, and *If You're an Egalitarian, How Come You're So Rich?* (Cambridge, MA: Harvard University Press, 2000). See also Peter Singer, "Rich and Poor," in *Practical Ethics*, 2nd ed. (Cambridge: University of Cambridge Press, 1993) and *The Life You Can Save: How to Do Your Part to End World Poverty* (New York: Random House, 2009).

2. Iris Marion Young, *Justice and the Politics of Difference* (Princeton: Princeton University Press, 1990), chapter 1.

3. See, for example, John Rawls, *A Theory of Justice* (Cambridge, MA: Harvard University Press, 1971), 9; David Miller, *Social Justice* (Oxford: Clarendon Press, 1976), 19; Brian Barry, *Theories of Justice* (Berkeley, CA: University of California Press, 1989), 355.

4. An earlier version of these basic rights and obligations was given in Jean Harvey, *Civilized Oppression*, (Lanham, MD: Rowman and Littlefield, 1999), 101–104.

5. Jean Harvey, "Oppression, Moral Abandonment, and the Role of Protest," *Journal of Social Philosophy* 27 (1996), 156–171.

6. Interestingly John Rawls writes about at least one of the items mentioned above. In speaking of "the [natural] duty ... to show a person the respect which is due to him as a moral being, that is, as a being with a sense of justice and a conception of the good," he mentions two things: seeing the situation of others "from the perspective of their conception of their good" and also "being prepared to give reasons for our actions whenever the interests of others are materially affected." See John Rawls, *A Theory of Justice* (Cambridge, MA: Harvard University Press, 1971), 337. The second of these duties is much the same as the one argued for here, but I arrive at it as part of a more explicit analysis of what the moral life involves, and I emphasize the role of major power differences.

7. Jean Harvey, "Forgiving as a Moral Obligation of the Moral Life," *The International Journal of Moral and Social Studies* 8 (1993), 211–222.

8. Kai Nielsen, *Equality and Liberty* (Totowa, NJ: Rowman & Allanheld, 1985), 93.

9. Laurence Thomas, "Moral Flourishing in an Unjust World," *Journal of Moral Education* 22, no. 2 (1993), 93.

10. For more on what I mean by "moral subordination," see Jean Harvey, "Social Privilege and Moral Subordination," *Journal of Social Philosophy* 31, no. 2 (Summer 2000), 177–188.

11. Gregory Vlastos, "Justice and Equality," in *Social Justice*, ed. Richard Brandt (Englewood Cliffs, NJ: Prentice-Hall, 1962), 45.
12. Ibid., 47.
13. Ibid.
14. Stephen Darwall, "Two Kinds of Respect," *Ethics* 88 (1977), 36–49.
15. Vlastos, 48.
16. An earlier version of this point was given in Harvey, *Civilized Oppression*, 107–108.
17. Barry, 354–355.
18. Harvey, *Civilized Oppression*, 43.

6 The Irreducibly Individual: Authentic Social Justice

1. Thomas W. Simon, *Democracy and Social Injustice* (Lanham, MD: Rowman & Littlefield, 1995), 16–18.
2. Ibid., 18.
3. Ibid.
4. Consider, for example, Susan Moller Okin's influential work, *Justice, Gender, and the Family* (New York: Basic Books, 1989).
5. John Stuart Mill, *On Liberty* (chapter 1: "Introductory"), 1859.
6. Paul Fairfield, *Public/Private* (Lanham, Maryland: Rowman & Littlefield, 2005), 5.
7. Joseph Tussman, *Government and the Mind* (New York: Oxford University Press, 1977), 5.
8. Ibid., 8.
9. Ibid., "Preface", 5.
10. Ibid., 8.
11. Ibid., chapter III, "Government and the Teaching Power," 51–85.
12. Ibid., 8.

7 A Rich Sense of "Responsive Reflection"

1. Margaret Urban Walker, *Moral Repair: Reconstructing Moral Relations after Wrongdoing* (New York: Cambridge University Press, 2006).
2. Laurence Thomas, "Moral Deference," *Philosophical Forum* 24, no. 1–3 (1992); Elizabeth V. Spelman, *Inessential Woman: Problems of Exclusion in Feminist Thought* (Boston: Beacon Press, 1988), 178; Christine Koggel, *Perspectives on Equality: Constructing a Relational Theory* (Lanham, MD: Rowman & Littlefield, 1998), 8.
3. Laurence Thomas, "Moral Flourishing in an Unjust World," *Journal of Moral Education* 22, no. 2 (1993), 93.

4. Bernard R. Boxill, "Self-Respect and Protest," *Philosophy and Public Affairs* 6, no. 4 (Fall 1976), 69.
5. Bernard R. Boxill, "The Responsibility of the Oppressed to Resist Their Own Oppression," *Journal of Social Philosophy* 41, no. 1 (Spring 2010), 11.
6. Carol Hay, "The Obligation to Resist Oppression," *Journal of Social Philosophy* 42, no. 1 (Spring 2011), 21–45; see also her recent book *Kantianism, Liberalism, and Feminism: Resisting Oppression* (New York: Palgrave Macmillan, 2013).
7. Koggel, 142.
8. Lorraine Code, *What Can She Know? Feminist Theory and the Construction of Knowledge* (Ithaca, NY: Cornell University Press, 1991), 77.
9. Margaret Urban Walker, *Moral Understandings: A Feminist Study in Ethics* (New York: Routledge, 1998), 131.
10. Will Kymlicka, *Liberalism, Community, and Culture* (Oxford: Clarendon Press, 1989), 9.
11. Koggel, 127.
12. Ann E. Cudd, *Analyzing Oppression* (New York: Oxford University Press, 2006), 191.
13. Ibid., 192–193.
14. Boxill, "The Responsibility of the Oppressed," 11.
15. Ibid., 8.
16. Ibid., 7.
17. Marilyn Friedman, *What Are Friends For?* (Ithaca, NY: Cornell University Press, 1993), 196.
18. Ibid., 198.
19. Ibid., 190.
20. Ibid., 189.
21. Ibid., 189–190.
22. Eva Feder Kittay, "At the Margins of Moral Personhood," *Ethics* 116 (October 2005), 122.
23. Sandra Bartky, *Femininity and Domination: Studies in the Phenomenology of Oppression* (New York: Routledge, 1990), 22.
24. Ibid., 23.
25. Anita Superson, *The Moral Skeptic* (New York: Oxford University Press, 2009), 63.
26. Thomas, "Moral Deference," 240.
27. Will Kymlicka, *Contemporary Political Philosophy: An Introduction* (Oxford: Oxford University Press, 1990), 211, quoted in Linda Barclay, "Autonomy and the Social Self," in *Relational Autonomy*, ed. Catriona Mackenzie and Natalie Stoljar (New York: Oxford University Press, 2000), 56.

28. Ibid., 55.
29. Ibid., 56.
30. John Stuart Mill, "On Individuality, as One of the Elements of Well-Being," *On Liberty* (Indianapolis, IN: Bobbs-Merrill, 1956), 71.
31. Ibid., 74.
32. Hay, "The Obligation to Resist Oppression, 21–45.
33. Claudia Card, "Women, Evil and Grey Zones," *Metaphilosophy* 31, no. 5 (2000), 509–528.
34. Koggel, 127.
35. Card, 509–528.
36. Robin S. Dillon, "Toward a Feminist Conception of Self-Respect," *Hypatia* 7, no. 1 (Winter 1992), 52–69.
37. Ibid., 57.
38. Ibid.
39. Ibid., 64.
40. Trudy Govier, *Social Trust and Human Communities* (Montreal & Kingston: McGill-Queen's University Press, 1997), 243.
41. Ibid., 251.
42. Ibid., 257.

Index

Lightning Source UK Ltd.
Milton Keynes UK
UKOW06n1823100415

249444UK00004B/79/P